TO

_____

FROM

_____

DATE

_____

WHEN
less
BECOMES
More

MAKING SPACE FOR SLOW, SIMPLE & GOOD

EMILY LEY

THOMAS NELSON
Since 1798

Published in Nashville, Tennessee, by Thomas Nelson. Thomas Nelson is a registered trademark of HarperCollins Christian Publishing, Inc.

Published in association with Folio Literary Management LLC, 630 Ninth Avenue, Suite 1101, New York, New York 10036.

Photography by Gina Zeidler and Ashley Cochrane.

Thomas Nelson titles may be purchased in bulk for educational, business, fund-raising, or sales promotional use. For information, please email SpecialMarkets@ThomasNelson.com.

ISBN 978-1-4002-1128-9
ISBN 978-1-4002-1929-2 (signed edition)
ISBN 978-1-4002-1129-6 (eBook)
ISBN 978-1-4002-1130-2 (audiobook)

Printed in China

20 21 22 23   DSC   10 9 8 7 6 5 4 3

To my girl. I love you, sweet Caroline.

CONTENTS

DEAR CAROLINE

Dear Caroline,

One day, when you're feeling stuck, I hope you pick up this book

I want to begin by telling you a little about who you are right now. You're four years old. You have the sparkliest blue eyes, the rosiest cheeks, and a strong body made for jumping, flipping, splashing, and dancing. You are loud. I'm not even sure you know how to speak at a normal volume. You say everything with boundless energy, enthusiasm, and expression.

You are delighted by tiny yellow flowers in the yard (weeds), being mommy's clothes helper (doing the laundry), and picnics (eating anything while sitting on the floor). When you tell someone you love them, you almost always do it with both hands on either side of their face, gently squeezing while you speak about one inch from their nose—your entire face squished into the happiest, most surprised "I love you so" face you can muster. You tell people you love them as if your heart may burst if you don't squeak the words out in this very special way.

You are everything good and *happy* in the world. I use those words on purpose. Not *great* or *magnificent*, because those words sound grand and maybe a little exhausting. You are pure goodness and light balled up tight into the shape of a little girl.

My prayer is that you stay this way forever.

But I am thirty-six. My mom tells me I was that same little girl as a child—unabashedly joyful. Now I have three children and a husband and a job. I love each of them dearly, but they keep me busy. I have laundry and a mortgage and a task list. And I wonder, *When did I begin to change?* I sometimes miss the girl I used to be.

You do not have to live life feeling stressed and burned out, Caroline. And if you're feeling that way now, as a grown-up girl, get ready to dig in. An unbecoming is ahead: an undoing, a nourishing, a filling up. I will walk you through my own journey from stretched-too-thin to unhurried and joyful in hopes that when you encounter this challenge in your own life, you will know wholeheartedly that you are not alone and that you were made for more.

Love,

mom

A SLOWER PACE

I pushed my double stroller down the sidewalk, following the same path as yesterday and the day before. Completely out of sync with the world around me (and with inconsolable angry cries coming from inside said stroller), I breathed deep and put one foot in front of the other. Have you ever felt like you need to yawn but you can't quite get enough air to do it? The subtle panic of that feeling mixed with stresses of work, family, and motherhood swirled around me.

Why is this so hard? I thought. Immediately the sour pang of guilt slapped that thought away. *Be grateful, Emily. You almost weren't a mother.* Shoving my feelings down, I pushed my chin up and kept walking. Hot tears stung my eyes, but I willed them not to fall for fear of what my neighbors might think.

My twins and their big brother filled my soul to its very brim, yet the day-to-day of working and mothering three children under four was difficult. The chaos, the busyness, and my own inability to "control" or organize this particular season of life into some kind of structure had sucked me absolutely dry. I was depleted and overwhelmed at the same time.

As I pushed these wonderful pieces of my heart down our street, I wondered if this is how it would always be. I was so in love with this precious life of mine, with so much to be grateful for, but so overwhelmed by what was required of me to do it all. I felt like a distant version of myself and wondered if I might be able to one day feel whole, creative, inspired, and joyful again. I trudged along like this, forcibly taking afternoon walks at the insistence of my best friend, who was convinced that moving our bodies was actually good for us. Apparently she was right.

What began with those afternoon walks was, in short, a slow journey from overwhelmed and empty to a new kind of full. I don't know if it was the sunlight, the endorphins, or the sense of being totally fed up, but walking outside, with my little ones, sparked something new in me. My frustration turned to determination as I gained strength of heart and body. One afternoon, I vowed that this would be the last day I'd feel this way. I was ready for a new beginning for our family. I was ready to find a better way. What followed was an upending of our frenzied existence and, eventually, a dedication to a life of less—fewer commitments, fewer distractions, and fewer self-imposed pressures to do it all. This slower pace and new margin in our lives eventually made space for the good stuff: simple meals together, slow afternoon walks, and sweet, unhurried conversations.

I slowly learned that less actually *is* more and that margin is magical. There is freedom from the frantic life the world tells us is normal. And there is so much goodness to be found on the other side of overwhelm.

RUSH

Less Rush, More Rhythm

Have you ever wondered when life began to be different? When did we change from happy little girls to frenzied women—perhaps even becoming frenzied moms of happy little girls? Where was that crossover? That time marked by stepping with one foot from the age of happiness and ease *into* the age of stress. Was it a specific birthday? Is there a mark on our time lines when we changed from carefree little girls into frazzled grown-up girls? Or was it a gradual shift in life and perspective that occured over the span of years, life events, and change?

Somewhere along the way, we went from thriving to surviving, from being full of joy to being full of stress. I believe this change starts to take place as we add commitments and responsibilities to our plates, never stopping to reevaluate or subtract as our plate begins to feel full. And as we rush to keep up with our overfull lives, we paradoxically begin to feel empty.

This empty feeling has a lot of names: *overwhelmed*, *stressed*, *frazzled*, *frenzied*, and *frantic*. While many treacherous and tragic things can cause us to feel this way, I want to dig into the idea of *everyday empty*: a state of being that happens when the enormity and momentum of everyday life begins to take over, taking up any space that could be left over for fun or joy.

> *Somewhere along the way, we went from thriving to surviving, from being full of joy to being full of stress.*

Many times, we allow our lives to continue at this pace because we are afraid to acknowledge the way we're feeling. We feel guilty for feeling anything but happy or grateful.

"Who am I to feel overwhelmed and empty when my basic needs are met—and then some?"

"Who am I to feel stressed and frazzled when I have healthy children or am cancer-free or am not dealing with XYZ like my neighbor or friend is?"

I've often shoved this empty feeling down into the corners of my heart because of the guilt that comes with acknowledging it. It feels as if, by acknowledging the overwhelm, I am devoid of gratitude for the blessings, privileges, and treasures in my life. So instead of identifying the problem and finding a solution, I have turned the other way and ignored the feelings, allowing them to fester and grow. This inevitably leads to a crash-and-burn scenario.

This large-scale burnout I feel so personally and see all around me is a tragedy and, quite honestly, a uniquely female epidemic. Our world is so much different than it was even five or ten years ago. My own mom marvels at what's been heaped onto the plates of young women today, including alarmingly busy schedules, social media, and constant connection through smartphones. The internet wasn't even around when my mom was in her thirties. The world is dramatically different, and I fear that we haven't done enough to prepare women to adapt along the way

Were we created to be pulled in this many directions, to be this "on" all the time? I certainly don't feel like I have the capacity for it all. And I know for sure that when I'm living life stretched this thin, I'm missing so much goodness along the way. *That* is the truest tragedy of this epidemic: the little ones rushed from activity to activity, the comforting routines of home life constantly interrupted by frenzied attitudes or rigorous schedules, and missing out on the true treasures of life found in ordinary moments—slow bedtime conversations with a toddler's head on the pillow next to yours, the way the sun sends golden rays through a big oak tree just before sunset, or the taste of crunchy buttered bread dipped into slow-cooked soup, made with love by hands that cared for your very first bite. Oh, what we miss when we rush through life.

THE PARADOX OF EVERYDAY EMPTY

Imagine that your life is a bright yellow balloon. As young girls, our balloons are adequately full of responsibilities, allowing space for joy. But as we get older, the balloons begin to change. It's not a slow leak that steals our joy. Instead, little by little, we add seemingly *good* things into it—one after the other. One more puff of air, followed by another and another. Job. *Jobs*. Marriage. A child. Children. Church. Volunteer projects. Social events. Social media. Phone calls. Text messages. Household chores. Mortgages. Soccer practice. Play practice. Tutoring. Meal planning.

A little puff. Followed by another little puff. Followed by just one more puff. Eventually, what happens?

At some point, the balloon either outright pops or it just barely holds, stretched taut, to its absolute maximum capacity. That "balloon" has become unfathomably fragile, susceptible to everything around it, ready to burst at a moment's notice. *This* is the paradox of everyday empty: a life filled to capacity with commitments, possessions, communications, and connections that is deceivingly full but soulfully and spiritually empty.

There is life beyond this. I challenge you to set aside

everything you know or believe about pouring out and filling up, about overwhelm and emptiness. Set aside the lies that self-care ends at a manicure and that the perfect organizer will instantly bring order to your overwhelm (yes, I just said that—and I make planners for a living). Becoming the girls God made us to be requires the tedious, difficult work of undoing, unbecoming, and unlearning until we are at our absolute basic self, then rebuilding, replenishing, and refueling our minds, bodies, and souls.

Oh, what the world could be if we all became those joyful, energized girls we once were.

BEAUTY IN STILLNESS

One December, in the middle of a very busy season of parenting and work, I took a business trip to Ohio. I knew it would be cold, but to my dismay, the weather forecast didn't call for any snow while we were visiting. I was bummed. At thirty-five, I had never witnessed an actual snowfall. I'd seen some light snow flurries and even a few snowflakes on a trip to North Carolina one time, but I desperately wanted to see white-blanket, winter wonderland–style snow. My travel companions had either lived in parts of the country that get snow or traveled previously to snowy destinations, so they weren't exactly on board with my snow-filled dreams.

Our first day was dreadfully cold and full of nonstop meetings, but we eventually turned in for the night at our hotel—exhausted and ready for rest. The next morning, much to my surprise, I pulled back the heavy blackout curtain to reveal the most beautiful Holiday Inn Express parking lot I had ever seen. It might as well have been Santa's workshop at the North Pole. It was glorious. Every car two floors below was covered in a thick layer of fresh, white snow. Out past the parking lot, the townhomes nearby were glazed with untouched powder as well. I squealed and immediately FaceTimed my kids to show them the beautiful scene.

I marveled at my first steps in the snow that morning as we all tromped to the car, surprised by how dry and fluffy the snow felt squeaking and crunching beneath my boots. When my coworkers and I got in the car, they remarked at how funny it was to watch me experience snow for the first time. They said I was like a little girl! And honestly, I felt that way. I can only describe my first snowfall as absolutely mesmerizing. For just a few minutes, the busyness and rush of our trip and all that comes along with leaving children at home faded away.

We drove through rural Ohio to the offices where we had meetings for the day. The snow was unexpected, so the entire town was quiet. As we twisted and turned through neighborhood after neighborhood, I couldn't help but marvel at the stillness of the morning. There were nearly no cars on the

I deeply, desperately, and quietly wanted God to replenish me.

roads, and everything felt strangely silent in some inexplicably beautiful, all-encompassing way I'd never experienced before. Every tree along the way—big, small, old, new, thick, thin, bearing thousands of leaves or none at all—was perfectly still and had been softly and purposefully kissed by the snow. The beautiful white flakes lay thick and still on every tiny and enormous branch, making the entire scene absolutely magical.

God didn't forget about a single tree that morning. It was as if He quieted the rush of the whole world to show us how much beauty can be found in stillness. He identified each and every tree, calling each one by name, and gave each majestic branch and miniscule twig its brief moment of glory as pure white snow was carefully and meticulously placed on it. I'd been feeling especially frenzied (after a cross-state move and busy days at work) and fought back tears at the thought that God hadn't forgotten me either. I didn't have a specific prayer I'd been hoping God would answer (other than for Him to bring snow, of course), but I deeply, desperately, and quietly wanted God to replenish me.

And so, God sent the snow. It was a reminder that God sees me, He knows my heart, and He knows exactly what I need. He knew that the quiet, magical snowfall—the brief escape from the rush—would be a balm to my tired heart and would remind me of how much joy can be found in stillness. In His own surprising, wonderful, snowy way, He reminded me of who I am (and Whose I am) and that the rush isn't worth it.

ENOUGH IS ENOUGH

Alabama has this song that always strikes a chord with me when I hear it. One particular lyric—about rushing to the point of life no longer being fun—is especially accurate. In my experience, that's exactly where rushing (to keep up with everything on my plate) takes me—to a not-so-happy place. Typically, this is a cyclical occurrence, the rush building up both quickly and slowly after intentional periods of calm, eventually pushing me to a breaking point.

Rinse.

Repeat.

Each time this would happen, I'd rework a few things in our lives, tinker with schedules and routines, and inevitably get back to rushing, hoping my solutions would permanently fix the problem.

I'm considered an expert on simplifying—I've even written books on the topic. But what I've noticed, with more years under my belt of strategizing techniques to automate, simplify, and organize the busyness of life, is that a deeper problem is at play in our frenetic, fever-pitched pace each day. A societal "way of life" has slowly crept in and become the norm. We can keep pausing the hamster wheel we're on to catch our breaths, but eventually we're going to have to step off.

While the tactics of simplifying daily life and organizing our time are incredibly valuable and life-changing, this insidious underlying epidemic bubbling just beneath the surface of our lives has caused them to fall out of sync and has bred burnout, stress, and emptiness.

So . . . what if we said enough is enough? What if we decided to live life our own way? What if we stopped racing toward this imaginary finish line? Could we walk instead? Could we settle in to where we are right now, acknowledge that "right now" is pretty good, and savor all we have to be grateful for? Even more important, could we proclaim that constantly pushing for "great" might not be worth the price we pay? What if, individually, we decided to take our lives back?

And what if we changed everything?

Our lives are so full, and yet many of us feel so empty. This paradox has confused me. If my life is full of good things, shouldn't I also *feel* full, whole, and joyful? Could it be that our lives are actually just *too* full? And that everything needs to be questioned? That perhaps there's a better or different way to live?

I began to wonder if less of everything might be the key. Maybe the world was wrong; maybe I could approach the rush and frenzy of our lives with the same tactics I used to organize and simplify spaces and schedules. When organizing a kitchen drawer, for example, you first declutter—by handling each item, evaluating it, and keeping only the best, favorite, and necessary. Then, once you've pared down to the essentials (the keepers), you add organization to it, such as a drawer divider or a system for sorting.

Life is the same way. We must first unpack our commitments, evaluate each one, and make a decision: keep the nonnegotiables and that which matters most, and then toss the excess. Only then, when our lives are clean slates and our commitments are what absolutely must and should remain, do we begin to institute rhythms and routines to help things run smoothly.

I know how to simplify my schedule, and I can organize a pantry like nobody's business, but this was new, deeper territory. What would it look like to reject modern social norms of living a constantly connected, overfull life and adopt a life that was a little less . . . and yet more? Could we turn down the noise a little? (I asked myself these questions as if I needed permission!) Could we slow our breathing a bit? What if we just sat still for a few minutes? Was it possible to settle into life in a way that was good, not grand? Could we intentionally seek out less? And was it okay to want that?

I began to have this conversation quietly with friends, as if it were an idea so outlandish that it should be whispered, for fear that someone might overhear and I'd be labeled as an extremist, or worse, *boring*. But what I realized as I talked to more and more people is that I wasn't crazy. I was saying out loud what others were having a hard time expressing. They were tired, plain and simple. They were overwhelmed. And they weren't happy. Everyone was trying to figure out how to take a breath. Life felt overly busy, fast, loud, and packed too full.

*What would it look like to reject modern social norms of living a constantly connected, overfull life and adopt a life that was a little **LESS** . . . and yet **MORE**?*

The more I talked to people, the more I became convinced that this type of life isn't working for any of us anymore. But what *would* work? The opposite? Quitting every optional thing in our lives? Clearing our calendars completely? Perhaps. Or maybe the answer lay in some gray area in between. Whatever the solution to this overwhelm was, I set out to find it.

QUESTION EVERYTHING

My first realization was enormous and foundational: our lives were not meant to include so *much*. The contemporary world has inserted so many additional and new things into our lives (puffs into our balloons), which we have passively accepted as perks of modern life. Many of these advantages didn't exist even a few years ago (social media, the internet, endless apps that can do anything and everything, to name a few), yet as humans, we still operate on the same level. We haven't adapted or evolved for this kind of massive shift. Sounds and colors and notifications and information come at us from every angle at all hours of the day. No wonder we're tired.

Add overwhelm and worry regarding daily activities—both of which are constantly running in the background, silently draining our personal batteries—and it's a recipe for disaster on both an individual and societal level.

I decided I would begin by questioning everything:

- Can we have good friends without attending every party thrown?
- Can we raise children of character without nudging them into every sport or hobby they show an interest in?
- Can we listen to stories on the way to school or work, instead of the news, and still be informed?
- Can we disconnect from our phones and social media and still be connected?

I began to examine how many toys we owned and the types of play I was introducing to my children. I looked at the setup of our home. Did it encourage our family to relax and connect, or was it too perfectly picked up and uninviting? I began questioning chemicals in cleaning products, fillers in children's snacks, and extra noise in our home. Digging deep into this topic became exhausting, so I created a manifesto for our family as a starting point. These statements would serve as guidelines for the decisions we make for ourselves, our home, and our children. As a place where we could begin to unwind and unravel years of adherence to what the world told us was right. In short, I wanted our family to live a life that was whole, good, and rich with meaning. And I was convinced that less of certain things would ultimately lead to more of what we all really want for our lives and our families: the slow, simple, and good moments worth cherishing and celebrating.

When we choose a value or an object, we unknowingly are

Less rush, more rhythm

Less liking, more loving

Less noise, more calm

Less distraction, more connection

Less frenzy, more soul rest

Less fake, more real

Less fear, more community

Less great, more good

Less chasing, more cherishing

Less stuff, more treasures

declining its opposite—even though the opposite may be the very thing we should be investing in or would lead to the outcome we most desire.

For instance, when we select a toy that lights up and makes sounds and entertains, we are essentially *not* choosing a toy that is basic and more play-based that would stir our children's imaginations. When we default to another night of dinner eaten on the run, we are saying no to a meal at home, however meager or simple it might be. When we spend hours scrolling through photos and updates from friends on social media, we are forgoing the undistracted time with our thoughts and with our people that would happen if we just put our phones down.

> We can say yes to a slower, simpler, quieter pace.

We can choose to say no to constantly rushing. We can say yes to a slower, simpler, quieter pace. When we opt for no radio in the car, we open the door for real conversation. When we say no to a second extracurricular activity, we pave the way for quality time with our kids, for rest, for refreshment.

YOU CAN SAY NO

The reality is that the world has changed and become more intense and fast-paced. We have allowed certain new complexities into our lives, further inflating our balloons. We have chosen to say yes to these things by not saying no. That's scary if you really think about it. But this realization can also be liberating! We get to *choose* what we say yes to. And we get to *choose* what we say no to. We have the ability to make these choices based on our values, mindfully adding and subtracting to achieve the outcomes we most desire. While we can't opt out of some responsibilities in our lives (going to work, parenting, paying our bills, etc.), there *are* some items on our plate we can say no to if we so choose. This realization excited me, and before I knew it, I was on a roll, questioning everything. The freedom that came with each small choice was infectious. And slowly, I felt the grip of overwhelm begin to loosen. Take a deep breath and walk through some examples with me:

You do not need a Facebook or Instagram account.

Oh, but I do, Emily. I need it so I can keep in touch with friends who live far away. But I use it for my business. I use it to share photos of our children for our extended family so they can watch them grow.

But do you *really* need to be on social media? Obviously, this choice isn't black and white. But what if there's a way to manage it differently that turns down the noise of social media just a bit? Options abound, such as scheduling business posts once a week or month, responding to questions and comments once a day, and limiting yourself to weekdays only.

You do not have to accept that social media is a three- to four-hour-a-day activity (or distraction) in your life. If your day is a pie chart, you get to decide how large of a slice social media takes up. Sometimes distractions (like social media) actually make our days feel more rushed than they really are because our attention is being constantly drawn away from what's happening right in front of us. It doesn't have to be this way.

Your kids do not need to be in dozens of extracurricular activities.

Oh, but they do. My children are interested in so many things. I don't want to stifle them. And you never know what interest might be "the one."

But *do* they? Which activity do your kids love most? What would happen if their focus was no longer on several different activities but solely on school, on one extracurricular, and on family? Could you introduce your children to other activities at home? With more margin and focus to dedicate, would their imaginations blossom? Would their creativity skyrocket?

In our home we've introduced "intentional boredom" (a very fancy term for taking away all the technology and shepherding our children into imaginative play). Embracing boredom in our home now paves the way for our kids to get creative: building forts out of pillows, crafting stuffed-animal homes out of cardboard boxes, or finding a sunny spot to read a book. This has decreased the rush of our week (with three kids, we now have three extracurricular activities per season) and increased imaginative play.

You do not need to be "that girl" who is always too busy for a coffee date with a special friend.

Oh, but I am that girl! I have so much going on. My circumstances are what they are. I just have to keep going like I am. Work, kids, house, laundry, meetings, repeat.

Trust me, I get it. But do you? Really? Are there ways you could add more rhythm and routine to the things on your plate you cannot remove? I'd venture to say that if you stopped and evaluated the hundreds of microcommitments surrounding your biggest commitments, you'd actually find quite a few things on your plate that you could adjust or say no to altogether.

Adding rhythm to your life is actually a simple task. We decide the cadence at which we live. We can add milestones or markers to our weekly and daily schedules to set the cadence for ourselves and our families. Implementing a morning or evening routine, for example, gives children (especially) and adults a sense of safety and belonging. They know what will happen next . . . and then it does.

The rest of the world may be frenzied and hurried, but inside the walls of our home, we follow a certain beat at night: dinner, cleanup, bath time, stories, prayers, bedtime. No evening routine is ever perfect, but this is the general goal. In the mornings we brush our teeth, get dressed, eat breakfast, clean up, and go to school. Our weeks are marked by fun, simple traditions like Taco Tuesdays and Pizza Party Fridays, as well as systems like chores, family values (posted for all to see), and rules for behavior understood by all.

These may seem like simple and obvious cornerstones of family life, but even as I write this, I can think of a few routines that could use either additional flexibility or structure in our own home. These ordinary routines and everyday occurrences are the *good stuff* of family life. And I can say firsthand that they are the first to be lost or sacrificed when the pace of life becomes too quick.

YOU CAN DO IT ALL . . . BUT *SHOULD* YOU?

We have a finite amount of focus and a finite amount of space in our brains. Neither of these is unlimited. *This* has been the single most revolutionary realization for me. You and the woman who existed a hundred years ago—before television and computers and the internet and smartphones and T-ball leagues and iCal— have the same mental capacity in your head. Her core focuses were different than yours are now, but she had a much smaller pile of things that required her daily thoughts and attention. You have hundreds, if not thousands, more.

That space in your head and heart is sacred. Protect it as

Protect the space

in your head and heart

as **HOLY**, and allow

only what's truly

and specifically

SIGNIFICANT in.

holy, and allow in only what's truly significant. This is where you must be brave. This is where it's easy to get stuck. We can believe the lie that we must do things the way we always have. We can believe we are powerless in our circumstances and therefore powerless against a future as burned-out women.

Or we can believe that God made us for more.

We can make choices that allow us to be women who have inner calm and outward joy. You were not created to be constantly overwhelmed. You were not created to function at max capacity day after day. You have not been forgotten. You are a daughter of the King, and you have the power to make choices about the way you live your life. You are precious and special and significant. You can opt for a life of less. You can say no to the world constantly telling you to be, do, and have more. You, like sweet Caroline, are capable of being a bright yellow balloon *adequately* full of *goodness and joy* whether you are four, fourteen, forty, or ninety-four. Destiny is a decision. So much in the world is out of control. But even if just a little we can manage what happens within the walls of our hearts and homes. This is holy work.

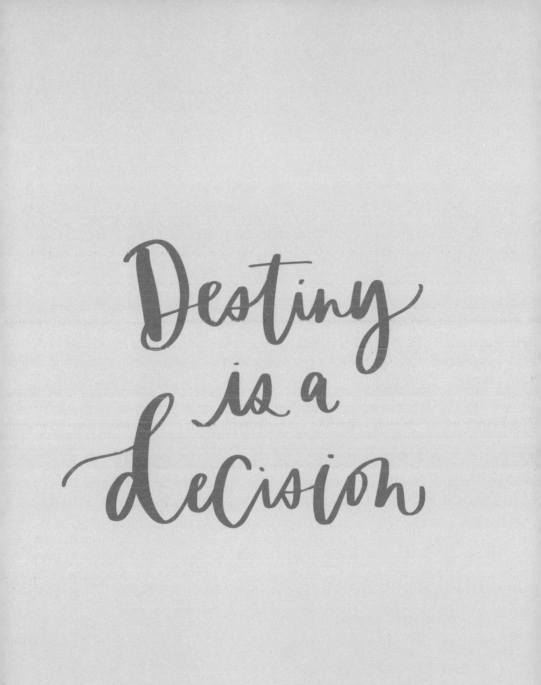

TECHNOLOGY

Less Liking, More Loving

I t was my husband who first pointed out the ways technology was both helping and hindering my life. Like me, he is an early adopter of fresh ways to automate and simplify. I'm usually what I like to call a "high-achieving multitasker" (which is a great thing, right?), but one evening, in late 2016, he found me crumpled on our bed. This was the evening of my pivotal crash and burn. This was the day "all the things" hit the fan.

No tragic event or anything terrible had pushed me over the edge, just a bad, full day. It was one of those days when, from the start, everything seemed to go sideways. The complications mounted and mounted until, finally, I crumbled under the weight of all I was trying to do.

Literally. I was in the fetal position.

Bryan's good at pep talks. He works in sales (and is really good at it) and is great at encouraging me, reminding me of my strengths, and kindly urging me to keep going. But that night? He flat-out told me to get up. It was time for some tough love.

"At any given moment, Emily," he said, "you have six group text messages going. You answer emails while cooking dinner. You voice-type messages while taking a bath. You even listen to audio books while blow-drying your hair."

> "You have to look at this with fresh eyes."

This was true. I would put in wireless headphones while I dried my hair.

"Why are you so plugged in? No one needs to hear from you that badly."

I was immediately offended. Deeply offended. Sure, if I were being honest, I could see the truth in what he was saying. But I wasn't ready to give in.

"When would you like me to answer my emails, Bryan? When I'm driving the kids to school? How about while I'm folding the laundry? Or maybe I should answer emails when I'm taking a shower."

My feathers were ruffled. And it wasn't that he was wrong. It was just that my balloon was overfull. The last thing I wanted to hear was that I should take something off my plate that I felt couldn't be removed. My life was a well-oiled machine with a thousand meticulously moving parts. If one tiny piece began to malfunction, the entire thing would fall apart. Or at least that's what I had told myself. This is how I accomplished so much. How I ran a big company and raised three kids and wrote books. My days were carefully broken into fifteen-minute increments. I knew that if I needed to take a conference call, I could take it at 11:24 a.m.—as long as it was no longer than six minutes. Because that's how long it took to drive to preschool to pick up the twins.

Yes, my life was that full.

Bryan sat down with me after my angry reply. (It's a good thing no items were loose on the bed, or I would have thrown them at him.) "You have to look at this with fresh eyes," he said. "You have to stop something. Something has to change. We can change our lifestyle. Do you sell the company and get a different job? Do we send the kids to day care? These are all options. Everything is an option. How do we get back to you being you? To the happy mom your kids love?"

That pushed me over the edge from anger into surrender. *Happy mom.*

My kids had seen a lot of tired, stressed, maxed-out mom for the last few months. Happy mom was in there sometimes, but my default was the opposite. I was able to fit so much into my days thanks to fancy technology like text messaging, email, and social media. Apps kept me on track and kept my world spinning. I thought I was thriving. I was so connected and plugged in. I felt powerful, really. I could take my kids to the park and keep running my business. I could "work" via text messaging, email, and apps while enjoying my kids. Sounds great in theory, right? But this kind of always-on work style can lead to total burnout.

REAL FACE TIME

Smartphones allow us to communicate with people without being face-to-face, which can lead to loneliness. In May 2018, *Fortune* magazine published a study conducted by Cigna, a large health insurance provider. Of their users, 54 percent reported that they felt lonely. How can that be in a world that is so overwhelmingly connected?

You're probably not surprised to know that 70 percent of Americans use social media. And many people claim they can't get off social media because that's how they communicate with friends, colleagues, and family. If that's the case and we're more connected than ever, then why are we so lonely? Could it be that we've traded true face time for FaceTime (or even just texting and emailing)? Have we traded our in-person communications or even phone calls for something more convenient but less personal?

THE BEAUTY AND BROKENNESS
OF THE INTERNET

I built my business on the internet and social media. We didn't have money to put into traditional advertising more than ten years ago, when Simplified was first founded, so I used my own personal social media profiles (and then later business profiles) to share content and news about what the brand was up to. Without social media I wouldn't be writing this book. Facebook, Instagram, and the internet are the connection tools I've used to create meaningful community around the Simplified brand.

While I've been able to observe and be part of the wonderful ways in which technology has connected the world, I've also witnessed the ways in which it has created a disconnect and even torn people apart. I've watched users publicly throw daggers at one another via comments. I've seen virtual strangers slap negative and bullying words on each other's posts. I had to get off social media entirely during the last presidential election. The vitriol and hate from all sides were just too much for me. I've watched division and divisiveness happen over and over again in 280 characters or less.

I've even been the subject of some of those comments. So have my children. And my marriage. And our home. I've read in the darkest corners of the internet that my creations are counterfeit, my message full of untruths, and my face not quite beautiful enough. Internet bullying has become so common, so unregulated, that children and grown-ups alike are targeted.

Why does this happen? Why do people behave this way online? Does it happen more on the internet than it does in real life? Is it because screens separate us, providing both shield and sword, making us brave enough to fight? Or because we cannot visibly witness the human emotion and reactions of the people we're communicating with? Is it because it's easier to be angry and opinionated and disrespectful and sometimes even evil online than in real life? Is it because humans as a whole are more overwhelmed and maxed out than ever before, so popping off a nasty comment or participating in untrue gossip is a bit of a backward release for an aching, stretched, sick-with-stress heart?

I'm not sure. But I do believe the internet is not the problem, just as phones aren't the problem for distracted parents. We choose to utilize these tools: smartphones, the internet, social media. And we can choose to continue or to leave them behind. Still, it all goes back to the heart. It all goes back to a broken world, full of broken people, in need of something that is not of this world.

On the flip side, I've been blessed to connect via the magic of the internet with real, hopeful, inspiring, incredible women all over the world. I've read stories of lives being changed by

The **INTERNET** is not the problem. Just like **PHONES** aren't the problem.

our products. I've met girls who've encouraged me and lifted me up, not just as the creator of a planner they love but as a dear friend they've come to know through little digital squares over the span of nearly eleven years. I've made friends. Real, live, in-person friends.

The internet isn't all bad. Neither is social media. When used for good and with responsible boundaries, they can be mighty, powerful forces for positivity in the world. They can unite and connect and provide. When overused or used for evil, they can divide, breed lies, and tear down. This is where we must be vigilant. We can't haphazardly allow social media into our lives or our children's lives for that matter. We have to be mindful and proactive about how we use these tools, what our values are surrounding them, and how we will govern their place in our lives—not *if* but *when* they become too much.

As with anything, even too much goodness from technology can be a bad thing. Imagine that woman from a hundred years ago we talked about in chapter 1. Imagine she somehow came to visit you today. She'd be amazed by quite a few new things. But imagine trying to explain to her what technology is and all that it can do. We can speak to a device on our kitchen counter that will turn on lights, set the temperature in our home, and read the weather forecast aloud. Little devices called smartphones can read us the Bible, track our daily exercise, and even teach us how to meditate. Our kids can use "tablets" to trace letters, listen to stories, and color pictures. From our computers and smartphones, we can order a gift to be sent to the other side of the world, video chat with a friend across the country, or read about absolutely any topic under the sun. How convenient! Yes, to a degree. But what are we missing out on in this connected, automated, technology-run world?

IMAGINE THIS . . .

You wake up, groggily walk to the chair next to your bed, and slip on your robe. Rubbing your eyes, you tiptoe barefooted through the quiet house to the back door, stepping out into the earliest light to feel the morning air on your cheeks. *Might be a good day for a light coat for the kids*, you think. The air is cool and just a little damp. You take a breath and head inside. A kiddo will come barreling down the stairs at any minute, so you quietly make a hot cup of coffee and sit down to savor at least a minute or two alone.

You pick up your grandmother's Bible, tattered and worn with age, use, and love. Along the margins, your grandmother left notes in her sprawling cursive handwriting, barely legible but still clear as day. You flip to the spot where you left off and start to read. It's not long before two of three kids are awake, and the book is put away again.

what are
we missing?

After school, you turn on some jazz music, your favorite, to set the tone. The mood is relaxed and happy. You lightly draw letters for your preschooler to trace on a few pieces of scrap paper. His chubby fingers grip the blue crayon carefully—and completely incorrectly. You smile and let him try his best for the last thirty seconds of his attention span. He draws something that somewhat resembles a *T*, and then you proudly hang it on the fridge.

At bedtime, your kids are rowdy. (What else is new?) To settle everyone down, you choose a story to read together. They select *Five Little Pumpkins* for the four hundredth time (even though it's long past Halloween), and you recite each page by heart, not even looking at the words. They're so proud to be able to narrate the book along with you. Practice makes perfect, you suppose.

A friend comes over a little while later, and over tea that you brewed and thoughtfully garnished with lemons and honey, you chat about life and motherhood and marriage and work. Afterward, you delicately wash the tea cups, dry them with a towel, and put them away. You change into your pajamas, wash your face, and apply a dab of hand cream. After turning a few pages in the book you're reading, you reach over to turn off the bedside lamp, close your eyes, and drift off to sleep.

Oh, what we miss when we let technology *do* life for us.

Imagine falling asleep without your phone plugged in by your side. Imagine an undistracted conversation with a girlfriend. Imagine softly singing your child to sleep while you stroke her hair and calm her heart. Could it be that there is beauty in a more analog existence?

NOISE

Less Noise, More Calm

Perhaps one of the most obvious ways that our lives have become overfull is noise. The noise level in my home at any given time (when all five of us are home) is astounding. I've often said that I'm noise sensitive.

A lot of noise means I can't hear clearly, think straight, or—to be honest—function well. I'm not sure if this is even normal, but noise drives me bananas. And I don't mean the kind of noise that happens when kids are playing or when everyone at the dinner table has something to say. I'm talking about the kind of noise that happens when electronics are buzzing, dinging, and chirping. Children are begging for attention, growing ever frustrated because their parents are focused on tasks or work or their phones. A scheduled practice or event is growing ever

WHEN LESS BECOMES MORE

closer, increasing the tension and the volume of voices and the directions being given. Thoughts are spinning and plans are being made to prepare for an overfull day tomorrow, expectations set high and patience running low.

And someone says they can't find their shoes.

And everything unravels.

The balloon pops, the last drop of patience has slipped through my fingers, and somebody snaps. Everyone is talking at once, no one is on the same page because everyone is distracted and multitasking, and the downward spiral continues.

Imagine this happening in homes all across America at the same time.

This is the worst kind of everyday stress for me. And it's an exact description of what happened in my home yesterday. It's happened a lot the past few years. I've tried different tactics for alleviating the noise that happens in these situations. Clapping my hands. Flashing the lights. Even yelling. Yep, I've yelled. More times than I'd like to admit. None of it works. The only thing I've found to work in these situations is to turn everything off. Turn off the television. Turn off the phones. Turn off the devices. Maybe even turn *yourself* off for a minute. Power down. Go into sleep mode. Unplug.

Because just like a device, if you unplug something for a few minutes, it will reset itself, restart, refresh—and be better for it.

TRUE SILENCE

Have you ever been in the middle of nowhere and experienced that eerie feeling when you realize how silent it is? No hustle and bustle of traffic, people, businesses, and more? It's strange, isn't it?

Bryan and I took an anniversary trip once to a golf resort in the middle of the state of Florida. We lost cell reception about thirty minutes before reaching the hotel (which, to be honest, had me both excited *and* a little frantic). Streamsong Resort is situated in an enormous old phosphate mine that has been converted into a golf course. It's hours away from any other city. I reluctantly left my cell phone in our room the first night when we headed downstairs for dinner. It's weird not being tethered to that thing, but it didn't work anyway and my parents, who were with our kids, knew how to get hold of us at the hotel if needed.

We stepped outside to walk across the property to the restaurant. I was immediately struck, in a jarring way, at the lack of noise. It wasn't that the place was just quiet; it was as if the noises that are usually present in my life had been sucked out of the atmosphere completely, leaving this void begging to be filled with something. The sensation almost made me anxious, like my ears were desperately searching for some kind of sound. But all I could hear was the *tap, tap, tap* of our shoes on the pavement. This extreme quiet didn't seem to faze Bryan.

But for me it was an out-of-body experience. I hadn't experienced that kind of silence in so long.

When working, I always had music playing in the background. When hanging out with our kids, the television usually sounded around us. When out and about, the noise of the environment acted as the soundtrack to whatever activity I was doing. But here there was none of that. There was nothing . . . except quiet. Apparently this resort had been designed that way intentionally, to give busy people a chance to relax.

So why was it so uncomfortable for me? I suppose my body had found ways to acclimate to the noise of daily life. But was that a good thing or a bad thing?

Bryan and I walked outside after dinner. The glow of the hotel was the only light for miles and miles. And it lit up only a portion of the sky. Looking up, I was once again unnerved by the contrast between here and there—what my eyes could see in this isolated getaway and what my eyes could see back home. *Here* the sky held hundreds of millions of stars, each one its own shade of white and silver and gold, each a unique size and brightness, carefully placed to make up this unbelievable blanket of sparkles. So many stars were visible to the naked eye that it almost looked unreal. Painted even.

Life can be so similar to that secluded starry night. When we quiet down, when we remove the excess and the noise, what's left is basic beauty. And not *basic* in the sense of "plain" or "average" but basic in the truest sense of the word: *fundamental*, of

When we **QUIET**

down, when we

remove the excess

and the **NOISE**,

what's left is basic

BEAUTY.

central importance. It's almost funny that the most basic things left in the sky once all the lights and flashes and billboards and airplanes and buildings are removed are the most beautiful stars I'd ever seen. It's a scene I'd never have been able to experience with all those other distractions and excesses around.

BASIC BEAUTY

Over the next few days, I found myself slowly adapting to the lack of notifications, pop-ups, advertisements, calls, texts, and emails. It was weird at first. I had become accustomed to jumping from topic to topic to topic very quickly in short periods of time. My focus could be on twelve different things in the scope of two minutes. Is that healthy?

If you think back to a simpler time, humans were tending farms or plowing fields. We were focused for long periods of time on milking a cow or pruning plants or harvesting grain or making and baking bread—interrupted only for mealtime or emergencies or some other human interaction. Even just thirty years ago, although the average American woman wasn't churning butter, her days weren't as driven by distraction. She may have had a cordless phone in the house, and the internet, if she had it, was likely dial-up. And cell phones were just a new-fangled idea for fancy people (and they sure weren't "smart"!).

These days, even a simple scroll through Facebook or Instagram can take you from a recipe for vegan egg rolls to the top ten ideas for a gender reveal party to political unrest in the Middle East and then back to thirty-seven photos of your second cousin's daughter's Bat Mitzvah. Wow. Even writing that series (taken, by the way, straight from my own Facebook newsfeed) is exhausting.

Were we made for this type of unfocused flittering? And if not, what are we doing to adapt or to care for our brains (and spirits) as they function this way? Could we walk away from this? Or could we slow the flittering just a bit? My new-found confidence, founded primarily in the gloriousness of the stars I'd seen and my thirst for more moments of basic beauty, said yes.

I began by unfollowing people on Instagram and Facebook. I value these platforms and obviously need them for my business, but I wanted to be proactive rather than reactive about the ways I use them. I decided that I would take the reins on what information I allow into my head and my heart. If you are my personal friend on Facebook, that means that you get a Christmas card from me. That's my litmus test. On Instagram, I follow only a handful of accounts chosen specifically and strategically to pour into my mind what I'd like to pour out. I have plenty of real-life friends I don't follow, for no other reason than that I'd rather catch up with them in real life.

TOO MUCH INFORMATION

Bryan and I went through years of infertility, rounds of medications, surgeries, and eventually in-vitro fertilization to conceive our three children. My best friend did as well. I recently remarked to her that infertility seems more common now than it used to be—and it very well may be. But she noted that, with the connectedness of social media and the internet, we are now more aware of others' stories than ever before.

In years past we never would have known of a young couple in rural Illinois who had to undergo complex treatments to have children. Or the couple in Washington who miscarried two babies before giving birth. The internet has made information (much of it from strangers or people only loosely connected to us) so much more readily available.

Now consider the number of positive stories you read online. They're heartwarming and wonderful for our mental health. But what about the sad stories? The bad news? The tales of sickness, disease, crime, and tragedy? In the past, we heard these only on the news or, going back even further, when stories were shared from a friend's mouth to your ear. Now? All we have to do is scroll a few inches down a newsfeed to take in dozens of these sad and scary stories from all over the world. Is that good for our minds and hearts? Should we do something to protect our minds from this input? To create a boundary or barrier for when too much has become too much? Compassion fatigue is another side effect: we see so much difficult news, for people we know only tangentially (or not at all!), that we can either sink into a pit or become totally numb. At some point, the endless onslaught of information can make it difficult to be present for our real-life friends because we're expending so many emotional resources online—and often without even realizing it.

I fear that if we don't create filters for the type of information we take in, if we don't set up boundaries to protect our emotional and mental energy, we are changing neurologically and feeding the monster of worry and doubt. We're adding gasoline to the fire of overwhelm and stress, and essentially feeding ourselves an unbalanced diet of "whatever the world throws at us."

If the adage holds true that we pour out what we put in, what does this say about how our social media usage affects how we parent, serve, communicate, and love?

DING, BUZZ, CHIRP, PING

I started to take note of all the noises and "pops" of information that zigged my attention one way before zagging it back

If the adage holds true that we pour out what we put in, what does this say about how our social media usage affects how we **PARENT**, *serve*, **COMMUNICATE**, *and* **LOVE?**

toward my actual area of focus. Many of these distractions were pretty obvious, but the big one that surprised me most was notifications on my phone. My phone would *ding* and *buzz* and *chirp* for every Facebook comment, Instagram like, email, text message, or app update. And because my phone was always with me, I always heard and noticed. These notifications seemed like a good idea . . . until they weren't.

Instead of sorting through which notifications would best serve me, I turned ALL of them off. Every sound, every pop-up, every red dot. Then I went back and turned on what I *knew* I needed (text messages and phone calls only) and left the others off. I'd still check my email during work hours, but I didn't get alerts every time one landed in my inbox. If something was urgent, I knew the person would call.

And it worked, as simple as that. I haven't turned a single notification back on. In fact, I eventually turned off my text "red dot" and told my friends and family to call my cell if they need me. Now I get to text messages when I'm able.

I also decided to address clutter, both in my house (which we'll cover in another chapter) and in my life. I began to say no to invitations I knew would stretch my schedule too much, commitments I knew would be a squeeze to fully dedicate myself to, and favors I just had no bandwidth for. I began to gratefully and unapologetically *decline* and to be proactive instead of reactive about what I allowed into my life—what I dedicated my time to. Little by little I carved out actual, true, better-than-gold margin in my days. "No" is a complete sentence. No apologies needed. As long as I was holding up my end of the core responsibilities, meeting the needs of my family, and fulfilling my duties as a boss and worker, everything else was actually optional.

I think we've underestimated the power of margin in our lives—time between responsibilities and commitments for life to just happen fluidly. I would argue that life happens in the margin, maybe even more so than amid our most important commitments. The free afternoon, the hour between appointments, even the fully unplanned weekend are when we find long chats with friends, slow meals savored with loved ones, and Lego creations built with hours of focus.

> *"No" is a complete sentence. No apologies needed.*

REWIRING AND REWRITING

These tactical ways of simplifying had always been the backbone of my company, Simplified. They're skills I'm innately good at and something I care for deeply. And I was a pro at putting them into place, but like any person, my life would get in the way and they'd unravel a bit (or a lot). It took constant dedication to keep life simplified and to keep my priorities in check. In late 2015, I'd created The Simplicity Challenge. It was

thirty simple steps to simplifying your life (primarily by clearing clutter, planning in advance, and setting boundaries) that went viral over social media. It was meant to be a New Year's challenge created to foster community among our followers and customers, but it became a sensation by which women around the world were changing their lives.

Now I see that although these tactical efforts are indeed valuable, they're just the tip of the iceberg. Digging deeper into the complexities of modern life has unearthed an epidemic so entangled and mainstreamed—the normalizing of constant busyness and chronic stress—that it can be addressed only by dramatically and wholeheartedly viewing the entire picture. And what better way to heal a marathon runner who's been sprinting at breakneck speed for years and years?

By allowing her to rest.

It's beautiful what can happen in that quiet space where we allow the body to still . . . the mind to still . . .. the heart to still. This is where God begins the wonderful work of rewiring our priorities and rewriting our lives.

QUIETING YOUR DIGITAL LIFE

Like it or not, our digital life is a reality that isn't going anywhere. Because of that, I find it beneficial to make mindful choices about how I interact with my devices and the worlds that live inside them. No one size fits all. Intentional choices that benefit you and put you in the drivers' seat are the goal.

- Turn off notifications on your phone and computer. I suggest starting by turning off all notifications and adding back only what is most necessary.

- Utilize the timer feature on various apps or your phone to limit your social media time. You may be surprised how quickly an hour on Instagram can slip through your fingers.

- Consider your goal for social media. Why are you using it? Create a personal philosophy of use so that social media serves your goals instead of you passively serving it.

- Streamline your inbox. Unsubscribe. Delete. Delegate.

- Activate your phone's Do Not Disturb feature. You can set hours each day when alerts and calls won't come through so you can focus on what matters: your family, work, personal goals, creativity, boredom, and more. Calls from your favorited phone numbers will always come through, but the rest will stay silent.

- Set aside screen-free time during the day—for you and for your family. Go outside. Take a walk. Read a book. Enjoy quiet time together.

- Let people know when and how you're available—and why. People are unable to respect boundaries they aren't aware of.

SOCIAL MEDIA

Less Distraction, More Connection

My realization about my connectedness and constantly unfocused attention led me to New Year's Eve 2018. I was exploring my smartphone's new Screen Time feature (a piece of software that measures individual phone usage) when I saw "5h 36m."

Five hours and thirty-six minutes.

That's how much time I'd spent on my phone the day before. Surely my phone had made an error. If I had been on my phone this long, surely it was due to December being the peak season for selling day planners. But as I scrolled back days and weeks and months, I saw that this was actually the average time I was on my phone *every day*. If I'm awake from 6:00 a.m. to 10:00 p.m., then this meant nearly a third of my waking hours were spent with this glowing handheld device in front of my face.

And I claimed I didn't have time to go for a walk? For a coffee date? To close my eyes and rest for a few minutes?

Oh, but I'm on my phone for business most of the time, I initially told myself. But since I was in the mind-set of questioning everything, I stopped myself. I thought for a minute. Was I actually on my phone solely for business? Or was I getting lost mindlessly scrolling?

I decided to acknowledge that, regardless, I wasn't happy with that 5h 36m and to dig in to the idea that perhaps, even if I use my phone primarily for business, this was too much—*and* that this connectedness (not the phone or the social media platforms or the internet in general) was contributing in some way, big or small, to my burnout.

I'd made some small but meaningful changes to my social media usage and to my phone, which is where I connected most of the time. But I had this glimmer of a feeling somewhere in the depths of my heart that this might go deeper. I'd squish it down, snuff it out. And like a tiny flame that wouldn't allow itself to be blown out, it'd somehow reignite, only to grow stronger and bigger each time.

The looming deadline for this book and a feeling of fed-up-ness pushed me over the edge. It was time to walk away. So for the first time in nearly eleven years (including during the births of my three children), I decided to fast from social media for one month.

The fast was simple to put into place. I posted that I would be taking some time away and explained that business posts (planned in advance) would continue to go up and that business-related questions would be answered by my team. If I only had personal accounts, I'm not sure I would have announced my departure. (I didn't say anything on my personal Facebook account, for instance. I just slipped away.)

The response to that particular post, which received thousands of likes and hundreds of comments of support in just a few hours, made me both excited and disturbed (a) that I wasn't alone in my feelings and (b) that the feelings of burnout and overconnectedness truly are more widespread than any of us realize. Tactically, here's how I began my fast in early 2019:

1. I posted on my business social media accounts that I would be taking some time away.
2. I deleted all social media apps from my phone.
3. I also deleted any *other* apps that took my attention away from actual face time with people.

Lucky for me, my frustration was at an all-time high, so the process here was pretty easy. I didn't make a big deal about it; I just walked away. I needed this break.

BENEFITS OF A SOCIAL MEDIA FAST

- Emotional bandwidth

- Fewer distractions and procrastinations

- Fewer privacy concerns

- Better sleep (if you check social media before bed or upon waking up in the morning)

- More time for family and friends

- _____

- _____

- _____

- _____

DOPAMINE EPIDEMIC

I'd love to tell you that this time away changed my life and my relationship with social media forever. But it didn't. In fact, although I thought this time of disconnecting would give me a reset and illuminate some of my bad habits, the time away actually revealed that I had pretty good habits with social media. I wasn't connected to it all day while working. I wasn't comparing myself to strangers on the internet in unhealthy ways. In fact, I missed some of my Instagram friends. I missed communicating with our customers. I missed the comradery we'd cultivated over the years with what we call our "Simplified sisterhood." I missed seeing photos of my friends' kids. I missed seeing updates from my kids' school. Social media really is awesome in the positive ways it connects us.

> *Social media wasn't the problem. My habits were.*

But here's the weird thing. As I continued tracking my daily phone usage through Screen Time, I found that my daily usage numbers weren't really going down much. I'd expected those numbers to plummet. *Social media is the problem, the thing that really logs the minutes that I'm glued to this phone, right?* But no. I realized something even more concerning.

Social media wasn't the problem. My habits were.

I was still reaching for this little device, both when I was bored *and* busy, during the day when I was chasing kids and at night when I had a few hours to myself. I was picking up my device, looking for something "live" or "continuously being updated," and silently asking it to fill my head and heart with something. To pick my phone up, out of habit, during my social media fast and find nothing there to entertain me . . . well, it was jarring. *What am I doing?* I'd think to myself. *Why am I reaching for this thing so often?*

I'm uncomfortable being bored or still, my subconscious would say to my smartphone each time I picked it up. *My mind has been trained to be constantly flitting from one thing to the next, and what's happening in real life right in front of me is a little slower than that right now, so please entertain me. Take my mind on a ride that's a little more interesting than Legos or work or paying bills. Pique my interest. Give me that shot of dopamine.*

Dopamine.

I guess I'd heard the word somewhere or read of the concept during some late-night deep-dive scroll into a *Scientific American* article. But it wasn't part of my daily vocabulary. Upon realizing that with each tap of my phone screen I was like a lab rat racing to sugar water over plain water, I became disturbed.

Dopamine is commonly called the "reward molecule." It's a neurological substance released by many parts of the brain

YOU MIGHT BE DOPAMINE DEPENDENT IF . . .

You find yourself aimlessly scrolling and tapping and opening tabs, looking for something to grab your attention.

You are a frequent user of the swipe-down feature to refresh feeds on your phone.

You find yourself engaging with online conversations you'd never normally pursue.

You open a social media app before even getting out of bed (or before going to sleep).

During real-life conversations, you have to resist the urge to pick up your phone.

that encourages us to seek, search, and even scroll, looking for some sort of reward or gratification. Social media feeds and smartphones in general are what researchers and marketers call "dopamine gold mines." By simply scrolling or flicking your fingers a few centimeters, you receive instant gratification (and therefore small hits of pleasure or fulfillment caused by dopamine) over and over and over again.

We experience the same spikes of dopamine every time we pick up our phones. Will there be a text message? Will we have a voicemail? A new notification? What will it be about? Maybe something exciting is in my inbox. Or some bit of news. That millisecond of "unknown" or "maybe" is fun for our brains whether we realize it or not. And we want more of it.

Dopamine.

Of *course* we keep coming back for more. In our fast-paced, too-full lives, when things slow down for even a few minutes, we reach for our phones. We even sometimes reach for our screens as a way to "rest" or to allow our bodies to do something "mindless." But it's actually the opposite! More dopamine, please.

I got kind of angry when I realized this. *You don't control my behaviors, strange neurological substance! I do!*

It also occurred to me that this behavior, this phenomenon, is happening to our entire society—this overconnectedness, this departure from real face-to-face moments, this dopamine addiction. It's real and it's an epidemic. And many of us don't even realize it happened. Some digital marketers and social media purveyors have begun to blend their business goals with some conscience, creating tools similar to the Screen Time software on our phones or the Instagram feature that alerts you when you're "all caught up" with your feed. These tools are a start—but they're only the beginning.

GUARDING YOUR HEART

As an entrepreneur, I think I am even more wired than most to seek out dopamine (and adrenaline, for that matter): the next exciting thing, the next interesting thing, the next new thing, the *next* thing in general.

Being content and slowing down is so unnatural for me. And this is what my month away from social media taught me: social media is not my problem. It's not causing me to burn out. But over the years, I have unknowingly trained myself to constantly seek out new after new. Hit after hit. Information and connection overload over and over again.

I realized this about midway through my month away and vowed to spend the second half of the month fasting not just from social media but from this behavior: constantly picking up my phone or opening a web browser to distract myself from the stillness in my head.

If my brain had been rewired over the past few years to

demand dopamine, I was going to have to rewire it now. Could I untangle the habits that kept me in overdrive and proactively train my brain with *new* habits (and boundaries) that would allow me to move at a slower, more focused pace? Could I learn to find contentment and stillness with less dopamine, with fewer hits of "new," with less distraction? I knew these things weren't helping me and that they certainly weren't contributing to the life I wanted—one that could find peace in a quiet afternoon watching my children play or sipping coffee while leisurely catching up on the meaningful parts of the day with my husband or dreaming big about chasing after what my spirit longs for most.

Because my business is on the internet and because my entire team works remotely, email, text messaging, and social media are vital. I wasn't planning to turn the clock back to the days of carrier pigeons, so I instituted some difficult-to-follow but eventually effortless tactics that I believed would bring me sanity and provide guardrails for those areas that I knew could be a source of struggle for me.

Instead of leaving my inbox open and allowing the "red dot" or some sort of pop-up to alert me when I had a message (what I call "working in real time"), I began to work with my inbox closed and kept all notifications turned off. (Again, if my children's school or a family member needed me, or some work situation was urgent, someone would call.) I adopted a work style known as batch scheduling, working creatively during the

Social media isn't our

PROBLEM.

It's not causing us to

BURN OUT. Constantly

seeking out new after

new is the problem.

morning and checking my email three times a day (morning, lunchtime, and in the afternoon before ending my workday). No longer am I slave to an inbox I'm watching fill up before my eyes, essentially a to-do list that others are creating *for* me (and that I'm passively allowing to dictate the details of my day). Now I set the schedule. I batch my email processing. I read and respond to emails at the time that works best *for me*.

No two days look the same. Situations arise that need more attention, and my inbox may sit neglected for a day. At other times, duty may demand that I'm engaged with incoming emails more frequently. Regardless, this type of focused, pro-active working has absolutely allowed my creativity to blossom. In fact, as I'm writing this book, my inbox is closed and my notifications are turned off. People have quickly learned that I'm not the girl who responds immediately to an email or text the minute it's received . . . and that's okay. I'm not the easiest person to get ahold of at a moment's notice. And that's okay. Because not everything is an emergency.

I realize this isn't workable for every situation and every job. But the concept can be implemented in small ways and still yield big results—and it can apply to more than just your inbox. Even if you can shut down your email for only an hour at a time (or put your phone on the coffee table and walk away), I guarantee you'll discover that the world will keep turning, that tasks will still be accomplished, and that you may just spark some creativity that had gone by the wayside.

NO MORE FOMO

In early February, when I returned to social media, I had a fresh perspective. But more than anything, my depth of focus had changed dramatically. As jarring as it was to leave, it was almost just as jarring to return. For years, my "focus" had been on hundreds of thousands of followers, thousands of friends, my local friends, and my family. That's a *lot* to focus on. I'd set my sights on so much that I found myself looking out long past what was right in front of my face.

Removing the masses, even if just for a few weeks, allowed me to regain focus on my immediate friends and family. I could see and hear them more clearly. I had fewer distractions and divergent focuses and was able to concentrate my love and attention on the people who truly matter most. It was a beau-tiful sabbatical that reset my heart in so many good ways. Coming back, I knew it would be important to create new bound-aries within my digital life to proactively manage my connections in healthy ways.

> *My depth of focus had changed dramatically.*

Anyone I didn't truly miss while away from social media, I unfollowed (even more than I had already unfollowed in the previous chapter!). This left me with a small circle of people I considered actual friends to connect with—whether via the internet or in person. Unapologetically culling my feed and

Above all else
guard your heart
for everything you
do flows
from it.

PROVERBS 4:23

following only people whose words or images brought some sort of positive energy into my life made social media a pleasure for me again. And having fewer friends to follow meant my feed updated less regularly and I was less tempted by the "fear of missing out." It also meant what I was consuming online was *by choice* and *good for my heart*. Less digital junk food. More inspiration.

I removed apps I was distracted by, and some that I had deleted during my fast never found their way back into my life. And I continued with some of the more tactical steps to simplifying one's online atmosphere: I unsubscribed from advertisement emails that called my attention away from the truly important emails in my inbox.

I was often reminded throughout this process of the verse from Proverbs: "Above all else, guard your heart, for everything you do flows from it" (4:23). How could I be the woman I wanted to be—the wife, the designer, the boss, the friend, the mother, the writer—if I wasn't proactively protecting the wellspring of my life, carefully considering what I allowed into my mind and heart, and choosing what got to stay and what had to go.

If our hearts are wells that can be either empty or full, then as much as I could, I wanted to steer toward those choices that provided truth, nourishment, friendship, and rest.

With these simple changes (and a healthy dose of perspective having lived without for thirty-one days), I vowed to mindfully manage my connectedness, allowing my brain to find a new pace—a slower, steadier pace. Less screen time and more of time engaged with the world around me. Less typing and more talking. Less clicking and more connecting—*really* connecting. This allowed my heart and my body to begin to find true rest—real, rich, refreshing (and sometimes analog) soul rest.

And isn't soul rest what we're all looking for?

REST

Less Frenzy, More Soul Rest

W hat is *soul rest*? We know our bodies need rest. That's why we attempt to get a good night's sleep every night. We know that when our rest is inhibited by a child or a storm or plain old insomnia, we perform at less than our A game the next day. Science backs this up. The deficiencies that accompany lack of sleep have been compared to being impaired by alcohol or some other substance. Bottom line: Our bodies and minds need sleep!

Now that my children are a little older, I get about seven to eight hours of sleep every night. After going through the experience of newborn twins, I can say that this is a luxury—and I don't take a good night's sleep for granted. But I wondered, as I continued to investigate remedies for my personal burnout, if *sleep* and *rest* are the same thing. We know that not all periods of sleep are equally beneficial to our bodies. In some stages of sleep, we are sleeping deeper or lighter, and our bodies therefore reap different benefits during different times.

SOOTHING THE SOUL FIRE

But what about rest? During most every stage of my adult life, the concept of taking a nap has felt absolutely frivolous and, to be honest, laughable. Most days I don't even have time to make my bed. Take a nap? Yeah, right. But with the discovery of lost hours during my day (hours given to mindless scrolling and searching on the internet), I wondered, *Would a fifteen-minute rest in the middle of the day do me some good? Are there other ways of giving my body and mind rest that don't equate to sleep?*

> *Are* sleep *and* rest *the same thing?*

When one of my children is abnormally fussy for a prolonged period of time, I instinctively know that he or she is overtired. Continually angry or ornery children almost always means, in the Ley home, that someone didn't get enough sleep. With tactics learned from my mom, I often soothe the soul fire (an unsettled or anxious spirit) of a cranky child by giving the others something to do, drawing a warm bath, slipping them into soft pajamas, and tucking them into a comfy bed in a dimly lit room. The gift of a nap (even if they go kicking and screaming) and some special one-on-one care can go a long way.

Why then, don't we extend this same kind of care to ourselves? Why don't we treat our own soul fires the same way? Why aren't we confronting our own cases of stress, overwhelm, and, for lack of a better term, fussy attitudes with kindness, self-love, and rest? Are we not also deserving of the same care we extend to those we love?

We're grown-ups. And many of us are mamas. We likely don't have a caregiver directing us to implement these remedies. But we for sure can choose to pour some water onto our raging soul fires ourselves.

And I'm not talking the kind of self-care that is going to get a pedicure or a massage. Sure, those things feel great and can be very relaxing and beneficial. The real, true self-care I'm talking about actually looks a lot like rest. Or better yet, soul rest. It's the kind of rest that soothes and quenches a hot, dry, thirsty soul—the kind of rest that replenishes our best attributes and draws us back toward our best selves.

This kind of soul rest is extra special. It may not always be found in lying down for a nap or hitting the hay early. I'd argue that this kind of rest is more unshakable, less likely to deplete or diminish quickly.

Soul rest may be found in the pages of a novel, drawing our minds into magical worlds, giving our imaginations a little room

Real, true

SELF-CARE

actually looks a lot

like **REST**. Or better

yet, *soul* rest.

to run free. It may be found deep in the middle of authentic, raw conversation with a trusted friend, one who truly sees and knows our heart and can speak life into our circumstances. It may be found, as my dear friend and coworker Whitney found it, in a garden—hands speckled with dirt, digging deep into the earth to coerce something beautiful from the ground.

Whitney (or Whit, as we call her) is a new mom. She has the tiniest, most precious little bundle of joy and works from home as creative director for Simplified. Whit has given me the honor of sharing her story, in her words, here.

A few weeks after finding out I was pregnant with our first child, my husband and I decided to plant a garden. I'd always dreamed of having a little garden to tend and care for—one that would provide veggies for our dinner table and flowers for the vase in our kitchen. I imagined myself walking out to snip blush-pink peonies every week to brighten our kitchen a little. Because I was a beginner, I spent weeks researching seeds and soil types, and eventually decided to build raised beds so I could tend the garden while pregnant and, eventually, with a little boy by my side. Together, my husband and I selected the soil, planted our seeds, and waited.

The morning of my induction, I woke with so much fear in my heart. David and I prayed that God would be with us through what was to come, giving us strength through all the unknowns. As I waddled from our home to the car to head to the hospital, I stopped in my tracks. There, along the driveway, in the beds we'd carefully planted, was our very first bloom: a pure white cosmos, dappled with tiny, sparkling drops of dew, standing tall and strong in the center of the garden. I'll never forget how proud I felt to have helped bring this flower to life. And surprisingly, it was pretty simple. All it needed was good soil, water, sun, and love.

A few hours later, all my hopes and plans for a smooth labor and delivery had been tossed aside. God and baby had their own plans for how this birth would go. It was unnerving and scary for this inherent planner.

After twenty-eight hours of labor, I held my precious boy for the first time. I never knew I could love something this much, *I thought.*

As we adjusted to our new normal as a family of three, my feelings were big and bold—and so was my exhaustion. It was unlike anything I'd ever felt before. I felt so different from the girl I used to be. The days were long and motherhood was hard. I longed for the strength and energy and vivaciousness I used to have. Thirsty for strength and renewal every afternoon, after long days home with our baby, I'd wrap my little boy in a baby wrap, tying him snugly against my chest, and head out to the garden. Sometimes I'd prune the flowers or tend the vegetables, but many times we'd just walk, listening to the birds and lawn mowers and frogs . . . sometimes just savoring the sweet silence.

Rob was soothed out there and so was I. The garden became our private place of soul rest.

As I looked out at my lush, growing garden and saw the bright blooms and strong stems, I was reminded that we as women need tending and care as well. Like my flowers, I need good soil (a firm foundation of rhythm for my life), water (nourishment from healthy foods), and light (from the sun, from truth filling my soul—the place from which I do my most important job—caring for the son God gave me).

I realized that, if cared for in the right ways, I too would bloom from the darkness I'd been feeling. So here I am, continuing on my quest to bring back the girl I used to be—both for my family and for myself. I'm remembering now just how strong I am and how worthy I am of a life well lived. It's as if the winter is fading, the North Carolina snow melting around me. I'm a little excited, reenergized, and ready to step into the warmth and sunshine after a long, cold season.

I found a lot more than peonies while digging and

*planting and tending the dirt and seeds just outside
my door. I found hope.*

What I love most about Whit's story is that it so beautifully illustrates the dichotomy of feeling two big emotions at once—overwhelming joy *and* paralyzing emptiness.

And I've talked with so many women from so many different seasons and situations in life who have felt this exact same way. We're not alone! Some have one child; some have none; and some have ten. Some work out of the home; some work in the home; some do double duty. Burnout isn't selective! We often feel as if we need more tools, more organization, or more time. But really what we often need is less: less noise, fewer distractions, and less comparison. So often we glance over at another woman who appears to have more on her plate and believe the lies that our feelings and experiences suddenly don't count. Emptiness can lurk in the shadows of your life no matter how seemingly complex or simple it is. Guilt and comparison love to keep us isolated.

Whit's feelings of burnout and overwhelm appeared amid a long-awaited season when her heart was brimming with gratitude for her little boy. She felt isolated and shameful for feeling anything other than pure elation—confused at feeling both empty and full at once. By slowing her pace and digging in to something life-giving, something that provided true soul rest, Whit experienced renewed energy, peace, and refreshment in

her soul and in her home. By slowing down to connect with something that might seem unproductive to the world, she opened herself up to the richness and peace she needed during this time of joyful and challenging transition.

Soul rest looks different for everyone—cooking, cleaning, reading, writing, running, hiking, painting, gardening, you name it. What might seem tedious to you is another woman's deepest joy—and vice versa. Soul rest activities are the things you can lose track of time while doing. Quite often, it's that activity that makes you begin to breathe a little deeper, pulling your attention and thoughts from the worries and monotony and stresses of the day, and relinquishing control to an experience bigger than yourself.

It's not always easy to discover what it is that brings us our deepest soul rest. But based on my experience, it's often right under our noses, something we don't even need to think hard about to find. Maybe it's kind of silly and we're afraid to admit it (drawing or coloring with our kids? taking a hip-hop dance class? writing poetry that no one will ever read?). Leaning in to these things that we often call "silly" or "extra" in our too-serious, overfull, don't-have-time-to-play world can provide us all *kinds* of true rest.

When was the last time you just played? Like literally played a game? A board game? Or even engaged in some kind of sports outside? Knees dirty and sweat dripping down your face . . . Laundry buzzer going off, but you don't care because kickball is way too important right now. Science reveals that breaking away from the monotony of day-to-day life to do something that inspires creative thinking, ignites a bit of a passion, and encourages laughter is actually really good for you.

FEEDING THE BIRDS

My kids and I feed the birds a lot. Maybe it's a maternal thing. I get a lot of satisfaction from feeding those little pigeons at the park. Sometimes I'll pack a few baggies of fruit and cheese, grab the kids' water bottles, pick them up from school, and take my little ones downtown. We'll park the car and walk about a mile to the end of the pier in town. It's a safe street since the road is mostly used for boat docks, not a lot of cars going up and down it. My kids don't have to stay tethered to my hand. They skip and run, and we make our way down to the end of the street where hundreds of pigeons perch in large, unexplainable groups, just waiting for someone to come by with a stale piece of bread. Here we sit and snack while we toss pieces of crust high into the air in the hopes that some swooping pigeon will snatch it up.

It's such a simple thing, feeding the birds.

But my grandma did it with me.

And now I'm doing it with my children.

We get some exercise. We're together. We're present in

those moments. Plus the vitamin D and extra steps don't hurt a bit either. Sometimes soul rest doesn't happen with our heads on a pillow. Sometimes we're filled up just by creating a new tradition or tapping in to what our bodies and hearts actually need. Doing so unravels anxiety and brings new life to the driest of seasons.

WELLNESS

Less Fake, More Real

The many steps that followed the evening I melted down in 2016 were just the beginning of my journey toward true health and wellness, the kind of whole wellness that would allow me to be the woman I desperately wanted to be—physically, mentally, emotionally, and spiritually.

First, I took myself to the doctor to determine if a long period of postpartum depression, undiagnosed anxiety, or any other medical issue might be playing a role in the way I was feeling. I wanted to get a baseline—to understand exactly where my body stood in terms of overall health. (I *highly* recommend taking this important step to invest in your self-care. I know it's easy to prioritize work and kids and many other things before yourself. Plus, no one wants to go to the doctor. But it's important.)

My doctor ran routine blood work, which revealed that I was prediabetic. This was incredibly alarming, as I was at a healthy weight and eating a healthy diet most of the time. Blood work also revealed that I was suffering from more than one autoimmune thyroid disease. The prediabetes was apparently caused by my constantly skipping meals, which caused my blood sugar to spike and crash consistently. And my autoimmune health had likely been triggered, at least in part, by difficult pregnancies and chronic stress. These revelations, especially the "chronic stress" part, pushed my desire to be truly well from something that felt good and superficial to emergent and necessary.

BECOMING WELL

The topic of wellness seemed more prevalent than ever—in news headlines, articles all over social media, and grocery stores suddenly stocked with a variety of new healthy options—so I had no shortage of articles to read, books to pore over, and friends to talk with about how best to nourish my body. I'd neglected it for so long, sacrificing my physical health on the altar of work and motherhood. I'd skipped meals (often working right through breakfast and lunch), indulged in one too many vices (sugary snacks or a glass of wine with my husband after a jam-packed day), and neglected moving and strengthening my body (I hadn't exercised in years—who had time for that?).

I knew that to get myself from who I was now (stressed, overwhelmed, and generally unhealthy), I would have to define who I wanted to be. So, I decided to clearly name the outcomes I desired.

I desired to feel healthy.

Chronic stress had done a number on my body. I wanted to have energy and life again. I wanted the bounce back in my step and the thirst for adventure back in my heart. I wanted to be able to run with my kids without being winded and crashing afterward and to have energy to do the work my job required. I didn't want to have to *drag* myself outside for walks or force myself to stretch. I wanted my thirty-something body, the body that had carried three children (two at once even!), to feel as strong as I knew it could be.

I desired to look healthy.

I almost didn't write this one down. It felt vain and possibly something that might be categorized as unimportant. But I didn't like how I looked. What looks healthy is different for each of us, and I knew in my heart of hearts that I was not healthy. It was time to be honest with myself and to stake my claim on what I wanted: to *look* healthy and rested. I wanted clear skin; rosy cheeks; bright, refreshed eyes; and strong muscles.

I desired my attitude and spirit to exude *light and love.*

I wanted to be filled with laughter and lightness so I could pour the same out in return. I wanted my mental state to be flexible and optimistic. I didn't want to live on the edge of impatience and frustration.

Tall order, I know. You may be thinking of some similar major changes you'd like to make as well—and feeling just as overwhelmed as I did. I wasn't looking to go from drab to fab, or to fit into any pre-kiddo jeans; I wanted *me* back. I realized that *this* is where the refueling, replenishing, refreshing part of the journey really begins to unfold.

If we want to be our best in the very busy marathon of life, we have to train like athletes. So I made some decisions: I would choose going outside for a walk when collapsing on the couch sounded more fun (and more doable!). I would choose a large glass of water instead of another coffee when just a *little* more caffeine felt like what I needed. I would choose to push back against my habits to become the woman I wanted to be.

This thought kept running through my mind and motivated me the most:

This is who I want to be.

On the inside . . .

On the outside . . .

I want to exude . . .

And here's why . . .

What better perspective to exemplify for my daughter and my two sons than that I was not the sum of my doubts? That I am more than my default actions? I am who God says I am. I am not a bad cook. I am not always "tired Mom." I am not selfish for taking care of myself. I am strong. I am not forgotten. I have every right to choose to love myself.

HABITS THAT HURT

When was the last time you felt truly well? For so long, I'd lived my life with my head barely above water. To get my business off the ground, I'd sacrificed my health—literally. I'd commonly skip meals to devote endless hours to never-ending to-do lists, grabbing convenience foods to get through the day (even those packaged as "healthy" options). I would stay up late— really late—and then drag myself out of bed early to do it all over again. Coffee sustained me until dinner, and then when the computer was put away and it was time to settle in, my body craved carbs and sugar in fierce ways.

I believe my overfull plate is what led to a few of my hurtful habits. As I began to assess my daily life and looked at what I saw around me, I realized these vices and habits creep into the lives of *many* women in my age group and season: sugar, carbs, and wine.

I will choose.

I will choose this . . .	Instead of this . . .

Finding your way

back to you is where

the **REFUELING**,

REPLENISHING,

REFRESHING part of

the journey really begins

to unfold.

Just a Glass

It was a funny joke in the early days of motherhood: *Is it time for wine yet? Haha.* My girlfriends and I would have play-dates on Fridays that always involved a glass or two of wine and not-so-healthy snacks. It was our source of relief from the stresses of new motherhood. None of us had a problem with alcohol per se (or at least not that I'm aware of). We enjoyed this time together and would laugh about mommy wine time (I'm pretty sure I even had a set of napkins that said something like "It's Wine o'Clock Somewhere!")

But somewhere along the way, it started to feel . . . weird. It was so much fun to curl up on the couch and watch a movie with my husband and a glass of wine or to enjoy dinner and drinks on the town with friends, but turning to alcohol to relieve the pressures of motherhood (or life) never felt quite right to me. Don't get me wrong—I love wine. I love the culture of it, the history behind it, and the beauty of making wine. Bryan and I have even visited Sonoma, California, where some of the best wines in the world are made. But the "mom wine" joke was slowly becoming a cultural phenomenon that didn't sit right with me. It was my friend McKay who helped put my feelings into words.

In late 2016, McKay wrote out her resolutions for the new year: get more sleep, exercise more, eat less sugar, stop drinking. *What?* I hung out with McKay all the time. I was shocked that she wanted to stop drinking and yet also oddly proud of her. As she told me about her goal for the next thirty days, I became more intrigued. She explained that although she didn't feel she had a problem with alcohol and that nothing crazy had happened, she just knew that her life had a slow leak. For her, it had started after she had kids (I see this pervasive marketing to young women everywhere today, not just moms). It was a pinhole, but it was there. In the back of her mind, McKay had always wondered if maybe this cultural norm wasn't helping her be the woman she wanted to be. So she decided to quit.

McKay was nervous at first. How would she respond when others noticed the sparkling water in her hand at a dinner and asked why she wasn't imbibing? Would she feel comfortable joining the conversation when out with new friends with no rosé to calm her nerves? How would she unwind after a long day of work and parenting? McKay dug up strength she wasn't sure she had for a goal that wasn't driven by necessity but by a desire in her spirit. Forty was approaching, and she was ready to be her very best self. Deep inside, she knew alcohol wasn't helping to get her there.

Our oldest boys are best friends, so McKay and I talk often. I'll never forget a conversation we had where she told me about a recent beach vacation she'd taken with her husband and friends. Evenings included pre-dinner cocktails and bottles of wine passed around the table. McKay enjoyed herself and had yummy food and drinks but opted for spirit-free beverages.

She told me about how she woke with the sun every day, something she'd never done before, grateful for a totally clear head to enjoy the sunrise. She'd never returned home from a vacation feeling so rested either. She didn't set out to quit drinking forever, but now that she's gone nearly three years without a sip, she tells me she'll probably never go back. She feels more herself than ever before, not only because of the lack of alcohol in her life but also because she dug up the strength to do something hard for herself.

> *The cultural dialogue that moms "need" or "deserve" wine is dangerous.*

Who knew such a seemingly small (yet enormous) change could catapult a woman so quickly into her best life? Less indulgence led to more energy, clarity, and life for McKay. I'm so proud of her, and her story has inspired me to take a look at my own relationship with certain behaviors. The cultural dialogue that moms "need" or "deserve" wine is dangerous. Walking through a local department store the other day with Caroline, I spotted not one, not two, but three shirts promoting the idea:

- Mama Needs Wine
- Mom Hard, Wine Harder
- Raising Strong Girls—Send Wine, Lots of Wine

I've never been so grateful that Caroline doesn't yet know how to read.

What are we teaching our daughters with these phrases? That doing hard things requires a chemical depressant? That mothering is so hard (or that *life* is so hard) that alcohol is necessary? And why in the world do we find this funny? Everything about this messaging feels wrong. The fact that mainstream stores carry items with this kind of suggestion seems to reveal a bigger problem than most are acknowledging. It's not a statement or mind-set I want my children to think is normal or humorous. A glass of wine every now and then is something I enjoy. But the message that we need alcohol to thrive, in motherhood or in any role, is dangerous and damaging.

What if we focused on the things that bring more to our lives? That truly lessen our worries and fill our cups? The healthy and meaningful activities that calm our nerves, settle us down, and equip us to live our fullest lives—good, hard, and everything else? Can't we encourage women and moms to wind down and find rest in other ways? And for some of us, is it possible we maybe *have* developed too casual a relationship with alcohol? I think it's time for this conversation and for us to talk about all the many alternatives. More than anything, I think *we* should own the narrative—not retailers and manufacturers and whoever it is that's saying women need wine to cope with life.

I still enjoy wine. But watching McKay's journey has changed

When we're feeling tired

or worn out after a long

day, that's when we should

push forward down the

path of most resistance

by **ACKNOWLEDGING**,

addressing, and **DEALING**

with how we really feel.

my relationship with it. I'm careful now to make sure I'm enjoying it for the right reasons and at the right time. If my tank is feeling empty or I'm super stressed, that is not the time to pour a glass and dodge the real issues. Because skirting reality with a temporary buzz will eventually lead me right back where I started, sometimes feeling even emptier. We're wired to look for the paths of least resistance. But when we're feeling tired or worn out after a long day, that's when we should push forward down the path of *most* resistance by acknowledging, addressing, and dealing with how we really feel. I realize this message won't make a cute t-shirt, but, wow, can "leaning in" change your life!

I would be remiss not to acknowledge here that consistent use of substances of any type can lead to addiction. This is why I find this "mothers need wine" message so dangerous. No. Mothers need support, friendship, rest, nourishment, and soul care. Mothers don't *need* alcohol.

As McKay's friend, I watched her awaken somehow when she started leaning in to her life and pushing out the vices. Gradually, I watched her eliminate alcohol, reduce her sugar consumption, and begin to learn about what fueled her body. She became certified to teach Yoga Sculpt to share with other women ways to fuel their bodies and lean in to hard things. I'm so proud of her. And so inspired by her commitment to living her *best*—with less of what drained her and more of what gave her life.

Mama needs...
rest, soul care,
nourishment,
truth, and
friendship.

Sugar-Sweet

Let's talk about something a little less heavy . . . a little sweeter . . . but still a little (or a lot) damaging: *sugar.* And let's be clear: sugar and me are *tight.* Like BFF tight.

During the course of my research after seeing the doctor and discovering some of my own very real health issues, I became interested in learning about functional medicine and gut health. I knew that the food I put in my body could either help or harm my inflammation and overall health. I like to say that I am a healthy eater about 75 percent of the time. But once my kids are in bed? The pantry and I have an interesting relationship.

I.

Want.

Sugar.

My body and brain are tired, and the cravings are real. I'll eat junk that makes me feel great in the moment but like garbage in the morning. Two rounds of Whole30 (a popular elimination diet) helped me realize that sugar and carbs were inflaming my body and worsening the very issues my doctor and I were trying to treat. Sticking my face in a bag of snacks may have *felt* amazing and satiated a craving, but it wasn't improving anything about my well-being. It was actually feeding my auto-immune conditions and further sucking fuel from my tank. More sugar was leading to less health.

Even when certain foods or behaviors aren't helping our

health, these habits are hard to break! Especially when we feel like we "deserve" a treat or two after juggling multiple responsibilities during the day. But I began to wonder, *If I'm feeling like my body and mind "need" something, what might happen if I had a toolbox of remedies and healthier options on hand?*

This is going to sound elementary, but I literally made a list of "supplies" for my new toolbox:

- a hot bath with my favorite bath salts or a candle
- sitting outside in the silence
- listening to a novel audiobook while accomplishing a few chores (physical clutter = mental clutter for me)
- moving my body by going for a walk or stretching a bit
- enjoying a hot cup of peach tea with honey and lemon
- reaching for a bowl of fresh fruit
- sitting quietly with my journal and scribbling down whatever thoughts are swirling
- turning up the music and dancing it out with my kids for a few songs
- calling my mom or a good friend

If we listen to what our bodies are truly craving (beyond the stuff that isn't exactly good for us), we often know what we need. And it is usually within arm's reach: rest, connection, a good laugh, or even a listening ear.

GET MOVING

That whole "get moving" thing? Suddenly I had a new best friend named Endorphins. I had been a dancer for fifteen years while growing up. When I graduated high school, I stopped dancing and exercising altogether. I did nothing (oh, the metabolism of youth!). Fifteen-plus years later, I knew that if I wanted to feel better and feel more capable of living my fullest life, I would need to move my body to gain strength inside and out.

So I took my life savings to a local gym and hired a trainer named James (he was about to become the friend who introduced me to Endorphins). James was strong and funny and full of energy. I was tired, terrified, and totally out of my comfort zone. But for one hour three days a week, James slowly and sarcastically brought me back to life. He wasn't one to be inspiring or transformative in his words. Instead he laughed with me, showed me the mechanics of strength training, and challenged me when I said I couldn't, wouldn't, and didn't have what it took to do the next exercise.

Over time, I got stronger. I could run longer, lift more, and muster up more stamina. As time passed, this equated to me being more excited about going for walks with my kids, more capable of throwing them in the air in the pool, and more energetic when those mid-afternoon slumps hit. I was fueling my body with nourishing foods, avoiding sugar and wine as escapes (but I refuse to deprive myself entirely of my beloved

Self-Care Toolbox

What positive, healthy tools could I reach for during times of stress or when my life feels overfull to the point of exploding?

Goldfish crackers!), and paying more attention to what made my body feel strong and healthy versus what made it feel weak, tired, or sick (milk, for instance, never quite sat well with me, so I opted for alternatives in my coffee).

I became more intuitive about my body and my health, and that's where the real change took place. I was slimmer (less swollen and bloated), felt fresher and more revived (my eyes, nails, and hair appreciated more water so much!), and felt happier and peaceful more often.

Endorphins are magical things. They are chemicals released by your brain when you move your body. They create that "I can do anything!" feeling you get when you're all sweaty as you cross the finish line. I strangely started to love getting sweaty. This was weird to me. I'm prim and proper and like to be "put together." But I started to love getting sweaty and working with my hands and putting my body to the test. I loved the way I felt with the music turned up loud, my hair piled on top of my head, and my body being pushed.

During those workouts, when the moves got hard and the repetitions became too many, I fought like crazy to push through. I remember even getting emotional (which is kind of weird when a Macklemore song is blaring from the speakers) as I felt buried anger and doubt and frustration I'd pushed down for a long time suddenly bubble up as I pressed myself and chose the path of most resistance.

Why am I not enough?

Why couldn't I carry my babies full-term?

Why do I struggle with food choices?

Why couldn't we conceive on our own?

Why do I lose my temper?

Why am I so impatient?

It was as if God was giving me the opportunity to unload my soul right there on that gym floor. The physical challenge was tearing open a hole for my spirit to break through. As I finally let that pain surface, I'd push and push and punch those thoughts in the face.

I am more than the sum of my doubts.

My body is strong.

I have wonderful children.

I am capable and worthy of being the woman I want to be.

I doubt James knew everything that was going on in my head during those workouts. But he probably saw the emotion and fight in my eyes. Working out, even when I transitioned to exercising on my own, made me a new girl. In fact, moving my body and fighting through hard stuff was probably one of the single most transformative things I did for myself. Even though I usually dropped to the floor once the timers ended and the music stopped, I loved the feeling of going up against something hard and coming out the other side.

And guess what? I lost exactly *zero* pounds during that time, but my mind and body were truly transformed in immeasurable ways.

FAITH

Less Fear, More Community

My biggest prayer in writing this book is to honor my sisters whose lives look different than my own and to honor any of you who may feel as if you don't measure up to everyone else. It's my heart's greatest hope that this message reaches every woman, no matter your story, your background, or your current situation.

Whether you're a single gal in a tiny apartment in New York City or a grandmother walking the halls of a big empty home in Alabama, whether you are living the city life, doing laundry ten floors down when the quarters stack high enough, or spend your time vacuuming half-eaten French fries from the floor of your minivan; whether you're a college gal working toward a dream career or a girl fresh out of high school off to train to begin your job now; whether you're a mom with special needs kids or a bright, beautiful woman with special needs of her own; whether your paychecks are plentiful or your paychecks are spoken for before you receive them; whether you worship the God who I believe created this world or are unsure about your walk in any faith, *these words are for you.*

I say this because, as it relates to the topic of faith, I've always felt like a bit of an outlier. Like maybe I don't belong in some groups. I'm a Christian and I publish with a Christian publisher, but I've always wondered if my story fits neatly with other Christian writers in the world today. I don't have a child-hood of church camps and stories of Bible studies and women's groups. You see, although I was raised in a very faithful family, I was not raised in a church. In fact, while I've attended numer-ous churches and been involved in a few great ministries, I first joined a church only when I was in college.

So know that whomever you are, sister—whatever your background, your story, or your beliefs—you have a seat at this table next to imperfect, searching me.

LOVE THAT NEVER FAILS

When I was a little girl, my grandmother took me to our local Lifeway Christian Bookstore to buy me a big-girl Bible. My grandmother and I had a special bond, one that crossed generations and connected us as sisters in Christ. More than anything in the world, she wanted the rich, golden love of Jesus to live solidly and brightly in my heart. She knew that no matter what life might throw my way, this unwavering love would never fail me. It'd always be there, burning bright, when life got hard.

She was raised by a single mother in Montgomery, Alabama, during a time when there weren't many single mothers. Her mom, my namesake, was mannerly and motherly and Southern as can be. She worked shifts at the makeup counter at the local department store, selling skin care and lipstick to ladies who could afford far more than she. She raised my grandma on hymns and cornbread and lived a simple life caring for her girl. Like my grandmother, I wasn't raised in a church. Instead, my family found Jesus at the dinner table sharing stories of choices made and lessons learned, on the shores of the pristine white beaches of our hometown, witnessing the majesty of God's incredible creations, and in the stands of the local football stadium under Friday night lights, where we connected with others over sports and hot dogs. I found fellowship with girlfriends who helped me memorize Scripture and worshipped down back-country roads with my windows rolled down and mediocre voice cranked up high singing Chris Tomlin and Point of Grace.

I wouldn't change a thing about this. My family's legacy is grounded in connection, communion, and fellowship, wrapped in its own unique packaging. The love of Jesus was taught not

More than anything in the
world, my grandmother wanted
the rich, golden love of **JESUS**
to live solidly and brightly in my
heart. She knew that it would
always be there, **BURNING**
BRIGHT, when life got hard.

in a Sunday school classroom for me, but on my bed, knee-to-knee with my mom, reciting the words of the Lord's Prayer line by line, slowly building up my ability to recite the whole thing. It was in Precious Moments books shared with my brother at bedtime, learning about good choices and poor choices. And it was in learning to put others' needs before our own, actively loving and serving others in our community.

As I got older, I found that I wanted to dig deeper into my faith. Why did I believe what I did? What else was out there? How did these things come to be? I questioned everything (even reading stacks of books about other religions). I've asked trusted mentors hard questions. I've even shaken my fists at God during hard times. But the Lord keeps finding me. And I keep finding my way back to Him. It's funny how that works. And in me, He began to stir a thirst for deeper knowledge into the truths put forth in the Bible. I became thirsty for truths I could truly dig my nails into when life got hard, rather than reaching for what the world told me would make things better.

A broken engagement and a called-off wedding. Years of infertility. A high-risk pregnancy, then another. Marriage and parenting. Entrepreneurship and risk. A few health scares. At some points in my life, I have hit my knees and tried to recover every earthly way I knew how. All the kale and exercise and screen-free time in the world is wonderful. Books about hustle and fresh starts and getting after your goals can take you far.

But when you're at your lowest, down in the valley, there's

only one way out: to lay it all at the foot of Someone so much bigger than you. We can hustle and strive and try all we want. But without the missing piece . . . the central piece . . . the piece that ties the rest of it together with unwavering truth, we'll all fall short.

I've never read the Bible cover to cover, but my goal is to do it soon. Even so, nuggets of truth from its pages have buried themselves deep in my heart over the years, as anchors for my soul during the ups and downs of life. The following verse is a cornerstone of my faith:

> *"Do not fear, for I am with you; do not be dismayed,*
> *for I am your God. I will strengthen you and help you;*
> *I will uphold you with my righteous right hand." (Isaiah*
> *41:10)*

During the times in my life when I've been filled with fear, riddled with anxiety, this verse has given me so much hope. *Do not fear.* Maybe one of you needs to hear it. I promise you can trust these words: *I will uphold you with my righteous right hand.*

As smart, thoughtful, strong women, we believe the lie that we have to do life alone. We are solution-oriented, and we are fixers. When life is off course or full of more than we can possibly manage or we encounter a problem, we survey the landscape, gather our tools, and *fix it*. Here's the hard truth I've

I will uphold

you with my

RIGHTEOUS

right hand.

ISAIAH 41:10

had to learn: God doesn't need us to be fixers. God is waiting to take the burden from us. To make our loads light. But laying down our worries and concerns feels counterproductive, doesn't it? Shouldn't we be focused on finding a way over, under, or around these roadblocks?

God doesn't want us to work so hard. Yes, He created us with strong hearts and minds and the ability to move mountains. But He wants us to *first* lay it down. Get ready for Matthew 11:28–30 to knock your socks off:

> *"Come to me, all you who are weary and burdened, and I will give you rest. Take my yoke upon you and learn from me, for I am gentle and humble in heart, and you will find rest for your souls. For my yoke is easy and my burden is light."*

Look at the lightness God wants for us. "You will find rest for your souls." *Soul rest.* This verse perfectly encapsulates the fullness Christ has for us: rest, gentleness, humility, ease, light.

Yes, please. Let us lay it all down.

A COMMUNITY OF LOVE

Over the years, God has also stirred in me a desire for a larger faith community for our family to be part of. But finding this community seemed really big and scary. I felt a lot of pressure to find the perfect place that checked all the boxes. And I also felt pretty nervous.

Stepping out into this desire meant I would have to step *into* the uncomfortable and own the fact that I didn't really understand how it all worked, that I was going to be the new kid, that I was probably going to have to visit a few churches (maybe even *more* than a few) before I found the right one. But I did. And it was awkward.

I visited churches all over, none of them feeling like the perfect fit. I wanted to find a place that felt right for me *and* for my husband and kids. Until one day—when I ventured into a school cafeteria with a friend and met a bunch of imperfect people with big hearts for God. They didn't have the perfect building or the perfect programs (yet). But they were good people who loved God, and they wanted to love others in big ways. Their love for the Lord was really simple and special to me. And they welcomed everyone into their doors. No one even batted an eye at the fact that I was the new kid or that I didn't speak fancy church language (they didn't either really!). And so I brought my family. And slowly we became part of that community.

When we moved back to our hometown last year, I set out to find a new church home for our family. And God provided because I put one foot in front of the other. Last Sunday, our three children were baptized there. It was a moment like no other.

I've learned, as I continue to walk out the topics of this book in my own life, that the following truth is the fundamental part of learning that less is truly more. Jesus didn't pick and choose the most confident, well-read, best-behaved people to join His table. He didn't surround Himself only with the best Scripture memorizers or the ones whose church attendance was the most stellar. He chose the broken ones. The imperfect ones. The ones who doubted and asked questions. He chose the ones with histories, and stories, and struggles. He chose you and me.

> God doesn't need us to be fixers.

And if we keep choosing Him, even when it's not easy, we will discover more—more peace, more richness, more joy. Even when we are doubtful or unsure, He always chooses us—*always*. Despite our imperfection, our brokenness, our overwhelm; whether we meet Jesus in a sanctuary or around a dinner table or with a friend; whether we're sure of His promises or have a question or five, He chooses us. And He has so much more for us than we could even imagine.

BEAUTY IN BROKENNESS

One of the hardest concepts to grasp in my faith is that Jesus doesn't always immediately fill our emptiness or manage our mess. During certain seasons of life, I've fought with my faith.

Why, if God is Lord of all, does He allow bad things to happen? Why does He allow important prayers to go unanswered? Why does He allow my feelings to persist if He doesn't want me to feel this way? Why doesn't He give me some relief from the craziness?

Over time, looking back at seasons of grief or struggle, I've learned that sometimes God doesn't immediately patch the holes in our balloons. Sometimes He actually makes a hole bigger. In those moments He is reaching in and working inside us. Because a quick fix doesn't add up to lasting and true growth. And because this is when our souls are most changed, often even made stronger as we become who God wants us to be at our core.

Perhaps then, there is beauty in brokenness. Maybe God does His holy work here instead of perfect scenarios—using our insecurities, our imperfections, and our brokenness to force us to slow our steps, to turn our hearts upward, and to be still. It's when we stop and lay down all the mess, when we finally unburden ourselves of all the things that are weighing us down, that we can turn our open palms upward and allow God to steward us into becoming the women He made us to be.

8

PARENTING

Less Great, More Good

Over the years, I've thought a lot about the kind of life I want to give our children. Bryan and I have always known we wanted to give our kids lives that are close and connected. We want them to value family and to find comfort in the connection between the five of us. We want them to know that home is always a place they can come to for a big hug, a listening ear, and a place to be still.

As I was on this journey to pare down and focus on what truly matters, Bryan and I talked together about how to define the family life we truly *wanted*, the life we dreamed of, the life we would invest our hearts in, not just what we didn't want.

We started by making a list of words that describe what we were after in our home and family, words like *comforting*, *peaceful*, and *connected*. And we frequently came back to a word that sort of surprised us both: *good*. Something about *good* just stood out to us so much. And I tripped over it every time I read it. Why did *good* feel so strange and yet also so calming to claim for our family?

Good felt so ordinary, like it should be off-limits for being too small, not great enough. Ten-year-old Emily or even twenty-year-old Emily surely would have written the word *great* or *successful* for what she wanted her life to be.

Why was I stuck on *good*? And was it okay to want this kind of life—a life of good? Was a good life less than a great life? Should I be striving for a life full of accolades and achievements of the trophy variety? Or was it okay for us to work toward a peaceful home, to keep a steady pace, to quietly cultivate a loving marriage, and to set our sights on fostering good character and kindness in our children?

Could it be that those good things actually add up to a life that is pretty great?

RICH, SLOW, MEANINGFUL

In a world of constant comparison, it's easy to believe we aren't measuring up to everyone else—that our children aren't as well behaved, that our clothes and cars aren't as current, that our homes aren't perfect enough, that our incomes are lacking, or

What words do we want to define our family life?

WHEN LESS BECOMES MORE

that our aspirations as women and as a family aren't sparkly or big enough.

I think we all know deep inside that these aren't what add up to a life. But they're the measuring stick we see around us every day—online, in magazines and books, on TV. It's difficult not to compare ourselves to that! I'll tell you that the more I have written, the more I have poured out my heart during this season and mined the depths of my dreams and goals, the more I have become convicted of just how damaging this comparison game is. And I keep coming back to *good*.

I want more good, less great.

Sometimes good is beautiful . . . and great can be a little exhausting. Sometimes good feels like a job well done . . . and great feels like a job never done. Sometimes good is full bellies and happy smiles around a table of paper plates and sandwiches . . . and great is the complicated monster of a "perfect" meal that stole our joy before we even sat down to eat it. Sometimes good is a staycation full of slow memories . . . and great is that overplanned vacation that wasn't relaxing or fun.

This shift doesn't mean I want to give up my career or stop dreaming big or stop working toward goals. It means that we, as a family, want to live a life that is rich, slow, and meaningful—in the ways that matter. We want to build a life that doesn't have to be the greatest or "the best." It means we are learning to develop a thirst for more exploring and more stories, fewer television series; more helping mama make cookies,

Could it be that

GOOD things

actually add up to a

life that is pretty

GREAT?

less perfect meals; more patience, fewer overscheduled days; more proactive intention, less reactive hurry. I consistently ask myself: *When I'm eighty and look back on my life, what will I feel happiest about? What will I be glad we did?* I'm fairly certain the good things are what will leave the most lasting impression and the deepest joy.

Instead of writing in order to create a bestseller, I want to write to really *reach* women in the most sensitive and meaningful areas of their lives, to move their souls, to inspire them, to help them a little and leave them different than they were. I want to give women permission to dream big—and dream doable.

Instead of trying to raise children who believe they have to be star athletes and valedictorians, I want to raise children who are hard workers, playful, inspired, inclusive, kind, and full of grace in their imperfections. Instead of striving to perfect my children, correcting every flaw and redirecting every misstep, I want to get down on the floor, put their hands in my hands, look into their eyes, and see them. And I want to guide them as a parent should . . . while giving their souls permission to be kids. More than anything, I want them to know that a good life truly is a great life.

> *Sometimes good is beautiful . . . and great can be a little exhausting.*

More Good, Less Great

In what areas of life have you strived for great? What might the good alternative look like?

Good	Great

PRECIOUS AND WILD

If I've felt burned out by chasing great, I wonder if my children have felt it as well? Just a quick scan of the news will confirm that tweens and teens in America are often deeply stressed and burned out by school and extracurriculars. But what about little ones? Have mine picked up on or even felt some of the anxiety and depletion I have felt, overwhelmed and exhausted by the world around them?

Bryan and I always laugh when we say that we thought for sure God would give us one child who was the "quiet one," the relaxed one of the bunch. We were *definitely* going to have one kiddo that tended to be a bit of a wallflower or more intro-spective and introverted than the others. We fought long and hard for our three children, the answers to many prayers said on knees sore from years of nightly pleas.

Our children are precious—and they are wild.

Every single one of them.

God didn't have any mercy on the volume level in our home when He gave us these three. They each have big personali-ties and lots to say, often at the same time. It's funny though, because they're each very introspective in their own way as well. They refuel by being quiet and alone—sometimes tucked in a chair somewhere reading or looking over the pictures in a book—even if it's forced quiet time. They think critically and deeply about things (right before shouting their thoughts and ideas). They have big emotions and love fiercely, which triggers heated disagreements at times. And they are some of the most creative kids I've ever met. I'm a big fan if you haven't noticed. They're just good kids.

But those big personalities, combined with our big personalities, make for one chaotic household sometimes. As the resident expert in organizing, planning, and simplifying, I've learned that rhythms and routines *absolutely, hands down* keep our world turning over here. They help us avoid tantrums. They keep the wheels on the family bus. They give our kids a feeling of safety and connection. And they help Bryan and me fit into our days all the tasks that go along with keeping a family of five running. Meal planning, calendar managing, laundry routines, shoe baskets, laying out clothes the night before—these things make a huge difference in our lives.

But as I've tinkered with and mastered these tactics in our home, I've begun to wonder more about the underlying factors:

- the need for systems and processes
- the beauty in the benefits of these systems

Why do cadence and rhythm and structure soothe my kids' emotions so much? What forces in our lives are these tactics counteracting? It's a simple equation really. If simplification and routine soothe my soul fires (fires stoked by burnout and overwhelm) and help me feel calmer, can we assume the same for our kids—that they may be experiencing mini-soul fires that could be tamped down in the same way? If x is a flurry of feelings manifesting from "too much" and too fast a pace for grown-ups and y is the peace that comes from structure, then x for our children—even if on a smaller scale and at different levels—must be equally soothed by y.

What it all adds up to (you're welcome for this math lesson) is this. *I think our kids are burned out too.*

This means childhood is in danger.

And that terrifies me.

There is magic in the inherent slowness of childhood, in being unburdened by grown-up worries and hurrying. So much of a child's mind and soul are developed during unstructured imaginative play and exploration like digging for earthworms, conquering dirt piles, and connecting the dots of creativity while wielding a bottle of glue and a handful of crayons. But what happens to these moments when they are enveloped or even swallowed up by rush, noise, distraction, and overscheduling? What happens to these moments, and what happens to these children?

> *There is magic in the inherent slowness of childhood.*

Our burned-out kids are missing out on the goodness of being little.

Although so many things outside my home are out of my

control, I can, even if just a little, control what happens within the walls of this house. If I, as the mother with an inherent skill and love for home keeping, can approach raising our kids with grace and simplicity in mind, then I believe we can save our kids' childhoods. We can proactively embrace less rush, less noise, and less chaos to allow more rhythm, more peace, and more play to live inside our home. So I set out to create a space and a cadence to our lives that honors our quest for the family life we want.

LEANING IN

A lot of my past anxiety was fueled by being at odds with the season of life I was living. I pressed against the joys of being young, childless newlyweds because we so desperately wanted a baby. I pressed against the craziness of having infant twins at home because it was so hard to juggle work at the same time. Everything changed when I learned to lean in.

I'd love to tell you that I learned to lean in because I had this incredible spiritual awakening. But really, I began to lean in because I was simply tired of the struggle. I started to weaken my grip on things: my need to control my children and their behavior, my need to keep a perfectly tidy home, and my fear that if I stopped hustling so hard, my business would fall apart.

It didn't. None of my fears came true. In fact, once I stopped pressing so hard against life, it started to let me in. I started to experience it more fully. And I started to learn to give myself heaps of grace.

My very first book is called *Grace, Not Perfection: Embracing Simplicity, Celebrating Joy.* The book you're holding in your hands is a continuation in my journey to allow more grace into life and, especially, into parenting. You are doing a good job, Mama. You can let go a little.

AN ACCIDENTAL EXPERIMENT

The Ley family happened upon an accidental experiment in mid-2018 when we moved into a rental home while our new home was being built. The rental was a thousand-square-foot beach condo that belonged to a friend. It was fully furnished and held many of that family's belongings for vacation trips they made to the beach. We had moved to our new city early and were living in this condo for three months so our kids could start at their new school at the beginning of the school year. This meant that we had to pack clothes, toiletries, dishes, and toys just for our time there. The rest of our possessions would be stored until the big move, once our home was completed.

I gathered three plastic bins with lids and let each child pack his or her favorite toys. Tyler packed his entire bin full of Magna-Tiles (magnetic blocks he uses to build elaborate castles and forts). Brady packed his entire bin full of all the Legos he could fit. And Caroline packed hers with sparkly princess dresses, shoes, and hats for dress-up. I snuck in a few coloring books and a box of crayons as well.

For the entire three months, my kids played with nothing else. They ran outside and got sandy at the beach, and they played with their bins when it was raining. They didn't have a playroom or even their own bedrooms to play in (in fact, all three shared a bedroom during our time there). They squeezed into the little living room, Legos and Magna-Tiles on every last surface, Caroline parading up and down the stairs in her Fancy Nancy shoes.

They played and they played and they played.

Bryan and I were flabbergasted at just how *happy* they were with a fraction of their normal toy and activity options. What about the stacks of boxes full of robots and kits and sets and light-up, blinking, motorized toys back in Tampa? What about the hundreds if not thousands of dollars that had been spent on all those toys? I'd simplified our collection of toys in years prior, culling the stash to primarily play-based toys, books, and items that inspired creativity and imaginative thinking. Still, simplifying down to just the favorites they had chosen for this season was a whole other level.

And yet they kept playing. For three months. With just those toys and each other.

I learned two huge things through this experience:

With less volume and fewer

bells and whistles,

our kids are getting

so much more—more creativity,

more **IMAGINATION**,

more interaction,

and more **JOY**.

1. My children don't need a lot of fancy toys and games to be happy and to use their imaginations.
2. My kids' attitudes and abilities to focus improved with fewer options and fewer decisions to make.

It was almost as if the kids enjoyed these favorite playthings more than ever before, figuring out new ways to use and play with just what they had. Instead of flitting from one toy to the next every few minutes, they made new creations, utilizing objects found around the house—an upside-down cup as a spaceship for the Lego guy astronauts or a series of shoes as a range of mountains for Magna-Tile cabins to inhabit. Every now and then, Princess Caroline would pretend to be a dinosaur and trample their creations, but for the most part, this was the most fun, engaged, and imaginative play I'd seen from my kids in a long time.

Essentially, our kids had two choices in our rental house: go outside and play or stay inside and play with the few toys they had. The television didn't get many channels, so we rarely turned it on. We spent rainy afternoons gathered around the white kitchen table, crayons strewn about, coloring books scattered across the surface. When it was sunny outside, we went straight out the door in search of sandpile adventures, seashells to collect, or an open space to kick a ball around. What more did we need?

When we moved from that rental into the home we live

in now, our living space expanded quite a bit. And as all the toys and possessions from Tampa were unloaded into our new space, into our fresh start, box after box . . .

Well, we saved the empty cardboard boxes and repacked some toys right back up to donate or give away. Funny thing is, our kids still gravitate toward the same toys they played with at the condo. And that's what we have out: toys to build with (Legos or Magna-Tiles), toys to pretend with (dress-up clothes), and toys to create with (crayons, glue, scissors, and paper). We have some board games tucked away in a closet, but otherwise, we've found that these toys support the childhood we want them to have. With less volume and fewer bells and whistles, our kids are getting so much more—more creativity, more imagination, more interaction, and more joy.

RELIABLE RHYTHMS

I'll be honest. Moving into this rental home unnerved me quite a bit. I was already nervous about moving our kids from one city to another, one school to another, and then from one home to another *twice* in the span of a few months. To help ease the jolts of those transitions, we decided to make sure we carried a few rhythms and routines from one home to the next.

In our old home, each of our children had a shoe basket that held their most-worn shoes and socks. They know to put

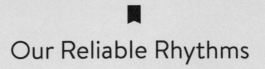

Our Reliable Rhythms

What rhythms do you and your family have that you can carry into times of stress or transition? What rhythms would you like to create?

their shoes away here and are able to put on their shoes when it's time to go. The baskets are easily accessible, always near the front door. Even though we had to cram the baskets under a console in the rental house, they came with us.

We feed our children breakfast at the kitchen bar every morning. We have for as long as I can remember. That time together, with Mom and Dad bustling about the kitchen, making coffee and filling water bottles for the day, is special and something they expect. So we were mindful to carry that tradition to our temporary home as well. We also made sure bedtime routines and Friday night pizza parties were on standby amid the transition.

These punctuation marks on daily life gave our children something familiar to cling to and fall back on when the rest of life looked different. They knew they could depend on these things. This put the emphasis on our family and traditions and off the building in which we lived.

WORN-OUT KIDS

I've witnessed, especially with our oldest, the ways that decision fatigue and overstimulation can deprive kids of the carefree joys and jubilation of childhood. This happens not just with toys and possessions but also with daily life activities. When parents are running at a frenetic pace, children often get overlooked.

One of the biggest conundrums here is a sentence I've said in my own head over and over: *I'm doing all of this* for you.

Our kids are asking for our attention and engagement in so many ways, as are our jobs, bills, relationships, and more. And so we say, yet again, that we're busy.

"Just a minute, sweetie. I'm tying your sister's shoes. I'll get to yours next."

"I just have to answer this email about your birthday party."

"Mommy needs to take this phone call from the T-ball coach."

And the underlying subtext is: *I'm cooking dinner and trying to write a grocery list and a meal plan for next week so you can be fed. I'm going in a million directions with soccer snacks and being class mom and more. I'm doing all of this* for you. *And no, I can't change anything about what I'm doing because without all this tedious work and feverish box-checking and planning ahead,* you wouldn't have this life you have.

Oof.

In this scenario, let's take a look at "this life."

Is this life for said child what we'd intended for him? (Full, yes—of activities and busyness.) Does he have the time and space to creatively and thoughtfully explore his eight-year-old world? To get outside and get sun on his freckled face, to dig with his hands and make worlds with bricks and rocks and clumps of mud? To track dirt across the floor while he washes up for supper? Does he have thoughtful, flexible boundaries guiding his path and choices? Does he have the time, freedom, and mental space to ponder his eight-year-old questions? (Why does a car make that sound when you start it? Why does water bubble when it boils?) Does he have the freedom to be bored, to be creative in his activities, and to play imaginatively? Is he able to lay his head on his pillow at night and spill out his heart, even if just a little, to his mom or dad, and then drift off to sleep having unburdened himself of big emotions?

Or is his little life *too full*? Is he being shuffled from one sport he loves . . . to another activity he enjoys . . . to play practice, which he seems to like? Is he, like us, too often spending his "down time" in front of a screen, all bright colors and loud, quick noises, scene-after-scene flashing in front of his eyes at a pace that is heart-quickening? Is he doing homework with the television buzzing behind him, electronics dinging beside him, and voices chattering in front of him? Is his sleep interrupted by worries and thoughts he's been unable to unpack with a parent who has time to listen? Is his little body being affected by preservatives and sugar in convenience foods handed from front seat to back during fast-paced mornings, hurried afternoon errands, and jam-packed weekends between birthday parties and play dates?

Are the expectations too high, the dependable rhythms too few, the noises too loud, and the pace too quick? Is his childhood being sacrificed for "all the things we must do"? What if we, as the grown-ups in this family unit, set aside some of "this

Are the expectations too **HIGH**,

the dependable rhythms too **FEW**,

the noises too **LOUD**,

and the pace too quick?

Is childhood being sacrificed for

"all the things we must do"?

life"? And what might that do for this sweet little boy? Is there a better way?

Could we allow him to be loud and make mistakes? Could we quit a few things and slow the pace just a little? Could we hold him just a little while while he gets the last of those tears out instead of reprimanding him for being emotional over something silly (like that his brother broke his Legos). Could we allow him to come home after a busy day of trying his hardest at school and behaving his absolute best and allow him to be his flawed, imperfect self a little? Could we honor the everyday imperfection in ourselves by gracefully and lovingly letting some things slide in our children?

What a world we could create if our children were loved with that kind of grace and patience! I fail at it every single day. But I keep coming back to this thought: *the work of bringing up kids in a too-fast, too-loud world is serious stuff.* It's hard and thankless sometimes. But the more I slow down, the more the "rewards" reveal themselves to me.

Maybe it's because our home is a little quieter or our days are a little less full, but I've found myself noticing things that were always there before but somehow are now right in front of me, in focus: the way Caroline pats her daddy's back during bedtime prayers, the way Brady still slips his hand into mine walking into school (those days are numbered, I know), or the way Tyler kisses my nose whenever we say goodbye or goodnight.

My goodness, those are beautiful things. Beautiful rewards and nuggets of goodness that get drowned out by the noise of the world when we believe more is more, when we believe great is always better than good. Beautiful rewards that, in a less-is-more life, become the high notes of the song, not the background noise.

Applesauce Muffins

Below is a special family recipe that my mom passed down to me. Applesauce muffins are the perfect simple comfort treat to share. They are best served warm, with butter, and can be frozen for future yummy breakfasts or snacks. They are a favorite around our home.

Ingredients:
- 2 cups applesauce
- 2 eggs
- 4 cups flour
- 2 sticks butter
- 2 cups sugar
- 2 tablespoons vanilla
- 2 teaspoons baking soda
- 1 tablespoon cinnamon
- 1 tablespoon allspice

Directions:

Mix butter and sugar together until well blended. Add eggs, vanilla, and applesauce. In a separate bowl, combine flour, baking soda, and spices. Stir into mixture. Grease muffin tins and fill a little over halfway full. Bake at 350° for 15-20 minutes. Serve with butter.

9

CHASING

Less Chasing, More Cherishing

Contentment is a hard thing to fight for. And I believe we must *truly* fight for it. Discontentment and constant "wanting" are fuel to the flames of burnout.

As humans, we are wired to constantly want more, bigger, faster, nicer. It's universal truth: we achieve something or acquire something, and then we move on to the next better thing. You've probably experienced the universal truth that goes with it: the next better thing never truly satisfies.

I believe God designed our hearts in such a way that only He can provide true, lasting contentment. Yet we (myself included!) work so hard to try to achieve that "perfect" life—the feelings of peace and happiness that accompany true satisfaction. You know the drill: we strive to reach "that life" by making the right career decisions, buying the right throw pillows, living in the right neighborhood, getting our kids into the right pre-schools. But then what? We want more. We're not quite there yet. We max out our credit cards. We max out our schedules. We max out our lives.

But when is enough enough?

This type of mental strain, in a modern world that's constantly telling us we can have and be more, is one of the fastest ways we burn ourselves out. With minds that are overfull, over-connected, and stretched thin, what happens when we add the "wants" on top?

I wish . . . I want . . . If only . . .

I can tell you that you're enough, that your life is enough, until I'm blue in the face. But I too know the stresses of discontentment. And I know that, until you're ready, no one's words will inspire you to sit in your mess, in whatever you might call mediocre, and find true, unabashed goodness.

> *But when is enough enough?*

These feelings of discontentment sometimes feel so normal that often we are blind to how ugly, entangled, and deeply rooted they truly are in our everyday actions. Consumerism is crushing. Perfectionism is pointless. We will never achieve a life that is totally, unendingly satisfying this side of heaven. And so, we must confront the wants and the chasing that spin quietly at the back of our

Consumerism is **CRUSHING**.

Perfectionism is **POINTLESS**.

We will never achieve

a life that is totally,

unendingly satisfying this

side of heaven.

minds day after day, whispering, *You aren't enough. This isn't quite good enough. You could be better, prettier, more successful. Your home could be nicer, fancier, more polished. Your marriage could be more romantic. Your kids could be easier, better behaved. And on and on . . .*

For me, staring these feelings in the face is like swallowing a giant mouthful of humble pie. And it doesn't taste good! I don't even want to admit these desires and struggles about *myself* in this book—that I too wish for bigger, better, and nicer.

But if we want to identify the causes of our overwhelm, we can't look at only the aspects of our personality or life we're happy to call out publicly. We must uncover the hidden parts of our heart that aren't as pretty. We must admit the ugly truth: the thoughts, feelings, and struggles we'd prefer not to claim. Giving these thoughts, feelings, and struggles a name, writing them down . . . this is the beginning of something good. This is where the journey of rewiring, healing, and undoing begins.

FINANCIAL "FREEDOM"

One might assume that financial freedom will bring ultimate contentment, but a lot of wealthy and broken people out there are evidence that that's not always the case. The deeper soul-wanting continues whether your funds are plentiful or few. Bryan and I are both college educated. We put ourselves through college and post-graduate school. We made our own way in the world, and we've both been successful. Financially, that's been great. We've gone from debt-ridden (student loans and credit card debt) to owners of several debt-free companies. It was hard. And it took a lot of sacrifice. But I think I've been afraid to acknowledge how financial freedom has affected my mind-set.

Early in our marriage, especially when we were working Dave Ramsey style to vigorously pay down our debt, funds were extremely tight. I can remember many times fumbling through dollar bills in an envelope at the grocery store, praying I had enough to cover that week's groceries. As the purse strings have loosened, we've become less thoughtful about our spending. We still stick to a budget for planning purposes, but we're quick to spend if we can fill a need, solve a problem, or better our lives in some way. And although this sounds ideal (and is surely a blessing I can't put into words), it has fueled discontentment. We're quicker to buy that sweater or those sneakers or that new bag . . . and then later realize that they haven't quite made us feel as happy as we'd hoped . . . and the quest continues.

This is a really difficult topic to talk about openly. Shouldn't anyone whose bank account rarely hits the zero mark always feel totally joyful and happy? Or could our money—and the accompanying privilege and ability to exchange it for the items we think we want—actually be hindering our contentment and holding us back in some way? Could this be a sign that we need to address our relationship with spending and contentment— that less stuff and less money might be the pathway to more peace?

I know this seems elementary, but even I find myself stumbling over the desire or reflex to add something to my life that I'm convinced will make me "happier" or make our life easier or better. In those quiet, reflective moments, I know this isn't true. I guess people wouldn't still be talking and struggling over something so "simple" if it wasn't also really, really hard.

Consider just how much time and mental energy you spend on the *chase*. A picturesque home. The best number on the scale. More fashionable clothes. A better television. A nicer car.

Level up. Level up. Level up.

Perfectionism can suck the joy right out of a perfectly happy life.

Advertisements, billboards, commercials . . . the outside world is constantly telling us that something bigger and better than what we currently have (or the way we currently look or feel or live) is out there, just waiting for us to snatch it up. Why *wouldn't* we chase it? We should always be growing and improving ourselves, right?

A few years ago, I would have told you yes, we should always be working toward a better life. But now, I feel like that strife is actually what holds so many of us back, drains us of our emotional reserves and mental energies, and distracts us from being truly satisfied in lives that are actually deeply good.

We chase great. We chase perfect. We chase more.

But do we ever get there? Or do we wear ourselves out on this hamster wheel, missing all the good along the way?

I think it's time to point our lives toward that place where *enough is truly enough.*

And what does *enough* look like? I'd challenge you, like I've challenged myself, to acknowledge that you may have enough right this minute.

Exploring this question—*do I have enough right this minute?*—has been game-changing for me personally and professionally. How many pairs of shoes do I need to own to be truly content? How many stuffed animals do my children need to feel truly loved? Instagram tells me I have to be a "boss babe" and to "hustle 'til it hurts" and to "achieve *all the things.*"

But what if I just don't? What if I live life just like it is right this second? Our needs are met, our home is great, our kids are clothed and fed. What if we all just quit trying so hard? What if when we quit trying so hard we suddenly find a richer and fuller life that we just couldn't see because it was covered up in so much stuff?

I don't need to boss or hustle or transform *anything* to be happy. I really think all I need is all I've ever needed—to just get still for a while, to just *stop* for a minute, to rediscover gratitude in a sacred way.

Have you ever taken time to sit down, quiet your heart and mind, and take note of everything around you? There is goodness in every mediocre detail. I promise you.

In the way your kids argue. *They are strong and brave.*

In the mess that sits at the foot of your washing machine. *My family has clean clothes to wear.*

In the frustration over meal planning. *We have food to eat.*

Why is contentment so hard to realize in today's world? Because our world doesn't want us to be content. Our chase for more has added to our discontent in more ways than one, which is exactly what marketing agencies and corporations want. How can one be full and content when "full" is never quite "full" enough?

HANDLE WITH CARE

When I was a little girl, I took special care in crafting beautiful cards for my mom, dad, and brother's birthdays. I'd thoughtfully fold construction paper in half, decorate with stickers, and cutouts and sometimes even glitter. In my sprawling, not-quite-right handwriting, I'd write birthday wishes on the outside and inside, before signing my name. I remember being so proud and excited to give them their cards. One even infamously proclaimed to my dad, "I love you more than peaches!" (truly a sentiment only my parents, who understood my overwhelming

I think it's time

to point

our lives toward

that place where

enough is truly

ENOUGH.

When Is *Enough* Enough?

Define the "good life" for yourself. What does true happiness and contentment look like to you?

affinity for peaches, could appreciate). This was just the way it was. Cards were always handmade. I try to remember this when birthdays roll around for my family.

Still, I've started to notice in our own financial journey that somewhere along the way, Bryan and I stopped being as resourceful. We started to simply replace stuff that had broken instead of working together to fix it or borrow from a friend. We bought convenience gifts instead of making gifts and cards. We one-click ordered books instead of going to the library. We had the means to afford things, so we swiped the card and checked the item off the list quickly.

Is something lost when we're able to do that with such ease?

As a kid, during the summer, my mom would take me to the bookmobile. The bookmobile was an old RV repurposed to be a traveling library. It would park in the Kmart parking lot near our house, and kids could enter, peruse the books, and check out a couple of their choosing. It was *so much fun*.

I think part of the reason I loved it so much was because there were so few books to choose from. I was a bookworm, so I'd take my time, choosing Berenstain Bears and later Nancy Drew, anxiously willing my mom to drive faster home so I could read them on our back porch. As soon as those books were thoroughly loved, we'd head back to the bookmobile for another round. It was in this little RV, in the experience of smelling the aging books and feeling their worn and tattered edges in my hands, that I fell in love with reading and, later, writing.

Today I buy my kids books on Amazon. They're delivered the next day.

Something is being lost here.

Is true joy found in the new and shiny, or is it found in cherishing the old and worn? What is more beloved: a cherished and cared-for heirloom or a brand-new item, tags just ripped off?

I think we all know the answer, but how do we cultivate more of this type of appreciation in our lives? The good news is that it doesn't require spending a dollar. Instead, it involves finding the beauty beyond "the next new thing," and cherishing true treasures.

TRUE TREASURES

We have a couple of treasures in our home, but the truest treasure that comes to mind is Kiki. Kiki is our youngest son's tattered, frayed, limp-with-love-and-use monkey that has been part of the family since Tyler was born.

Kiki, as Monkey is known, is a special member of our family. A gift from a friend, Kiki was once a plush, soft brown monkey with squishy arms and legs. These days, he's probably sort of sad-looking to most, a tattered and worn version of his previous

self, but he's loved dearly nonetheless. Kiki has gone with our family on every trip, to every doctor's appointment, and to bed with Tyler every single night of his life. He even spent some unexpected time in a UPS box (being shipped from a hotel where he was accidentally left behind).

Here's Kiki, fraying around the edges, likely looking like he needs to be put into retirement, And yet Tyler's many other stuffed animals aren't even on his radar. He only has eyes for Kiki.

What were we chasing when we filled Tyler's room full of those many unused stuffed animals—when he already had his beloved? Were we trying to make sure he knows we love him? That he isn't forgotten when Mom and Dad are away? Or were we trying to elicit a brief moment of joy and a few hours of happiness on a special occasion (something that usually ended with said animal being tossed aside, sadly forgotten, for months to come)? The reality is that a personal note from Mom likely would have created a more lasting impression. Some special one-on-one time (to run an errand together or to read just one more story at night) could have achieved the same, if not better, results.

A NEW KIND OF SIMPLE

When we have the financial freedom to afford modern conveniences, a lot of seemingly positive outcomes can happen.

Conveniences, services, assistance—all become possibilities in today's world with even marginal disposable income. And none of them are bad! Many, in fact, bring overwhelmingly positive benefits to people's lives. Having been the grateful end user for some of these services, I can't help but wonder what we might be losing by automating or outsourcing certain tasks. If we want to look at this from that perspective, then what services might we consider giving up for a greater outcome?

Dinnertime is always a struggle for me. Not only is it often "crazy hour" with kids who are growing tired and hungry, but cooking isn't my best talent. When we had infant twins and a four year old at home, and both of us were working very long hours, we started ordering pre-made dinners from a local service. During that season, it was a tremendous luxury and convenience. A few nights a week, dinners would arrive pre made, we'd heat it up, and eat. Easy peasy. Everyone was fed. But as life became less about surviving (three kids under four) and more about getting back to basics and really thriving, I started to question what we were missing out on continuing to opt for this convenience. I remembered washing lettuce with my mom and learning how to scramble eggs with my dad (low and slow). I thought about our simple dinners at home and the sound of Peter Jennings on television while something sim- mered on the stove.

Now we don't order dinner in as much. It takes commit- ment, but I'm back to meal planning on Sundays and spending

What if the scenic route,

the route with more

TWISTS and **TURNS**

and time, is

actually sometimes

the better option?

time with my kids in the kitchen. They've learned the art of scrambling eggs, how to set the table, and how to wash their own plates. Caroline loves to wash lettuce for salads while Tyler lays out forks just-so at everyone's place settings. Brady's bigger, so he helps stir soups or pull roasted veggies from the oven. I absolutely miss the convenience of having a few dinners delivered each week, but I've loved the joys of having my kids in the kitchen with me.

THE PATH OF RICHEST RESULTS

I've spent a large portion of my adult life asking the question: "Is there a more efficient way to do x, y, and z?" and then quickly adopting ways to automate and simplify. But I have begun to wonder if "simplifying" always equals "faster" and "easier," if the shortest route from point A to point B is always the *best* route. What if the scenic route, the one with more twists and turns and time, is actually sometimes the better option?

Could simplifying actually mean taking life back to its most basic core elements in some cases? What if the "simplified" option In this new kind of simple isn't always easier but is the one that enriches our family's experiences rather than helping us cram more into our days? What if choosing the simpler option sometimes means leaning in to the path of *most* resistance—the path that will yield the greatest, richest result?

I used to run to my local car wash to wash my car every other month or so. It was easy and automatic. But one day, as I sat there while the machines scrubbed my car, I started to remember summers as a little girl, helping my dad hand-wash our family minivan. It was hot and sticky outside, so the opportunity to use the hose was exciting and refreshing. We would take a five-gallon white bucket from the garage, pour some dish soap from the kitchen into the bottom, and fill it up with the garden hose. Thick bubbles built up really fast, running down the side of the bucket and down the driveway. My dad would spray down the car with water, then use a soft brush with a long handle to spread sudsy bubbles all over its exterior.

I was in charge of the tires. Using a soapy rag he'd given me, I would wipe in between every silver opening in the hubcaps, proudly scrubbing away every last speck of gritty black grease. My dad can't be serious for long—it's not in his blood—so he'd inevitably "accidentally" spray me with the hose at some point, and I'd blow bubbles off the palm of my hand onto him. When we were finished, the family car shone and sparkled like brand new. We were so proud of our work!

And I want my kids to feel that same kind of pride and slowness in doing a job together, a job that could easily be automated or outsourced . . . but that may have value beyond how quickly it is accomplished.

What I've discovered on this journey of simplifying and

automating then course-correcting is that we sometimes miss something when we opt for the path of least resistance, the fastest way from point A to point B. Taking an hour to wash the family car together—the "analog" option, the less efficient option, in this instance—means taking an hour from your day. It means saying no to something else in order to say yes to this time together, to focusing on a task (and having some fun) together. It means valuing the journey, the experience—possibly even more than we value the end result. We gain so much when we opt to savor life rather than speed through it.

So tactically, how do you approach the less is more philosophy day-to-day? It all comes down to that elusive thing we're all after: balance.

It's this ghost of an idea that we can someday have everything managed and operating perfectly in our lives. It's that thing we never really achieve. I've often said balance is like riding a bike. We lean left and right to stay upright and keep from face planting. Adopting a "less is more" attitude is the same. Some days, we find that washing the family car together would be a good activity, so we lean away from making dinner together (pizza night!). Some days we want to create memories with our kids by making lasagna together in the kitchen, so we run the car through the car wash. Some days work requires more of your attention than usual. So the kids get the joy of picking out a movie and popcorn to share at home. Some days work is slower, so we choose to read three bedtime stories to our kids.

Here's the kicker: you can't ebb and flow like that when your life is crammed full. There's no wiggle room for flexibility when your days are packed to the very brim. Embracing the more of less is about giving yourself grace as you lean one way, then lean the other—achieving the life you'd like to create for your family in the long run, not the short. It's when we focus on the short term that we fill our lives with too much and cannot thrive in the long term.

HOME

Less Stuff, More Treasures

For the year and a half that Bryan and I dated, before we were married, we lived eight hours apart. He lived in Tampa, Florida, and was pursuing a career in sales. He was the handsomest man I knew, clean-cut and dapper in a suit and tie every single morning. Bryan was driven, ambitious, and charming, climbing the corporate ladder, crushing sales goals, and thoroughly enjoying the city life. I was enamored with this fast, fun lifestyle that was so different than my own.

I lived in our hometown of Pensacola, Florida, at the time. It was small, growing, and quiet but was connected. Pensacola is part beach town and part quaint small-town-USA. Family was so important to me that I'd never considered venturing beyond the city limits.

One morning in early 2008, while visiting Bryan in Tampa, he asked me to marry him. I was asleep when he proposed. Sort of. He snuck into the room, gently woke me up, and asked me to be his wife. He said it was the only way he could surprise me—by practically asking me in my sleep. I was beyond surprised, and of course, said yes. We spent the next hour dreaming about our wedding and planning my move to Tampa. We were excited to be newlyweds in a city with so much life and opportunity. But we vowed to move home to Pensacola before we had children so we could raise them around family.

But life and kids and opportunities happened. Both of us were successful in our careers. Our kids went to great schools. And we'd made a great group of friends.

Still, underneath it all, something always felt off. Tampa never truly became *home*. Even though we sometimes talked about the idea of moving back to Pensacola, we knew we couldn't make a change because Bryan's industry didn't exist there. So about six times a year, we traveled home to see family. Our kids became expert road trippers. We lived in two places at once—spending holidays and special moments with family back home and living our everyday lives in Tampa. It was exhausting. But it was all we knew, so we kept going.

Then, in late 2016, while visiting my family back home, we ended up with a kid-free afternoon. We parked our car downtown and walked from a favorite restaurant to a wonderful

boutique coffee shop and then to the new brewery everyone was buzzing about, running into friends at every stop.

Something about Pensacola has always made me feel more like my actual self—and less like the girl I sometimes try to be. I'm rooted in Pensacola, and the city reminds me who I really, truly am inside. It's comforting and effortless.

On a whim, Bryan suggested we go look at a few open lots he'd seen. Moving didn't make sense at this time in our lives, but we loved real estate and would sometimes go look at houses or lots just for fun.

Before we knew it, we were standing on an unruly plot of land, shoes covered in dirt and stickers and sand, staring at each other with a knowing look on our faces. We were sup- posed to see the land, talk about how great or not-great it was, and move on to the next one. But in this particular space, on this particular piece of land, it felt almost as if God was stirring something inside us that we hadn't allowed to be disturbed. The sensation was weird and wonderful . . . and also like we had stepped into a moment we'd been destined for all along. It was almost as if neither of us needed to say anything. I was thinking it was perfect. He was thinking it was perfect. And it made *no sense* to either of us.

And that past-due promise we'd made ten years prior hung in the air between us.

This imperfect plot of dirt beneath our feet held more prom- ises than we could count. In some ways, the idea of moving home felt *absolutely right*. And in other ways, it absolutely did not add up. Bryan's career. Our friends. Our kids' friends. The house we adored back in Tampa.

Would we be stepping backward by moving from big, bustling city to smaller, sweeter town? Wasn't some kind of badge of honor associated with fighting rush-hour traffic every day and being amid a constant hum of activity? The Super Bowl was played right down the street from us in Tampa, and Pensacola didn't even have a Chipotle. What were we *thinking* considering closing a chapter on Bryan's thriving and stable career and exploring (and risking) him pursuing his own entrepreneurial dreams?

We could have labored the decision for months. So much was on the line and so many factors needed to be considered. But there, in that one afternoon, standing on this accidentally discovered plot of dirt, we decided to finally keep the promise we'd made all those years ago.

We made an offer on the land.

It was time to go home.

MORE OF LESS

Moving our family from a big city to our small hometown was quite an adventure. A *lot* of feelings were involved—for everyone. It was scary and exciting and hopeful all at once.

For nearly a year and a half, we crafted our forever home. We carefully selected grass cloth for the entryway walls to create feelings of warmth and welcome. We planned lower ceilings than the grand two-story ceilings in our previous home to bring the living space down a bit and create feelings of coziness. I decreased the size of my home office by over half so I could have a simpler workspace for my business, perfect for writing and designing. Materials chosen in soft shades of greys and blues were paired with hints of antiqued brass and weathered wood.

I had one very specific, non-negotiable request for our home: a long kitchen table, surrounded by windows, that could seat our entire extended family. To date, my favorite memory in our new home has been watching kids and grown-ups, friends and neighbors, all pile into our banquette to enjoy a meal. On one side is a bench, and surrounding the other three sides are chairs. There really aren't designated place settings, so everyone just kind of squeezes in. A giant pot of spaghetti is passed around, salad is dished out by grown-ups, and little hands reach impatiently across the table for another piece of bread and more butter.

This is the noise I've searched for all along. This noise, above the chirps of my phone and the dings of the computer, louder than the billboards on I-75 and the commercials on all three hundred TV channels, is the sound of the simplified life we dreamed of. This type of chaos is life-giving, not life-draining.

Home—no matter the size, shape, or style—is more important than ever. We made the decision to move our family to our favorite town for a purpose. Raising our children around family, creating experiences, and cultivating childhood at a slower pace was more important than anything else a city could offer our family.

And we sacrificed to get here, or so it seemed in the beginning. But now our schedules are more flexible, our kids are more connected, and our weekends are filled with potlucks, cookouts, and soccer games. Everyone here seems to know everyone, and there's a deep, abiding comfort in that.

Moving home was a big decision. And it was a calculated, planned, and beautiful one. We intentionally left a life that felt big, fast-paced, and upwardly mobile to embrace a different pace, a smaller community, and days full of the good stuff that comes with a small group of close friends and family. Now there's no place we'd rather be.

NOW MORE THAN EVER

In late 2017, I released my second book, *A Simplified Life*. The morning of the big day, I drove my kids to school and came home to prepare to make the announcement on Facebook Live. I've always been very interested in the ideas of home keeping—in organizing, simplifying, and making life at home calmer and more efficient. *A Simplified Life* covers ten areas of life that often become overwhelming for busy women and explores ways to cultivate home as a place of respite and rejuvenation.

But my mind was spinning that morning. Just a few days prior, at a country music concert in Las Vegas, a gunman had opened fire on a crowd of people, killing fifty-eight. I was consumed with worry over what had happened. What was happening to our world? Why were these tragedies becoming more prevalent? How in the world could I protect my children when totally unexpected horrors like this happened?

And who in the world would care about home keeping at a time like this? What did the rhythms and routines of family life matter when these kinds of things were going on in the world? Weren't there so many bigger things to worry about, to be consumed by, than life at home?

Like a jolt to my subconscious, I suddenly thought, *No. So many bad things are out there . That's a reality of life. So many things will suck us dry and challenge our safety, security, and faith in humanity.*

For those very reasons, the big and small things that happen inside the walls of our homes are more important than ever.

The feelings we cultivate in our living rooms.

The food we nourish our bodies with in our kitchens.

The bedtime stories told with patience and love.

The tired little heads rested on laps, hair gently stroked to soothe away the ups and downs of the day.

Home is where fullness begins. Home is where we are most replenished, refueled, and refreshed. It is inside the walls of my home that little personalities are nurtured, grown-ups are known and heard, and family bonds are forged.

Home is the place we go back to at the end of the day. It's where we retreat after work, play, and school. We've gone out into the world and done our thing, and now it's time to head back to home base—the place where we can relax, be ourselves, and sit and stay a while.

> *Home is where fullness begins. Home is where we are most replenished, refueled, and refreshed.*

Home is where we're fed and fueled, where we bathe, removing what's left over from the outside world, where we rest and rejuvenate. Our homes are holy places. Home should allow us to be in our most natural state, removed from all the trying, striving, and acting that happens outside its doors.

Home has the power to fill us up, with its board games, story books, music, Bible stories, hot cups of tea with honey and lemon, little (or big) piles of warm laundry. These monotonies of everyday life are the magic of the home.

A lot of love is involved in being the person (or people) who are actively cultivating a life-giving home (a term borrowed from my dear friend and mentor Sally Clarkson, author of *The Life-Giving Home*). I truly believe it's one of the most important, powerful things we can do: to create a home that nurtures the people who live inside it.

CRAFTING A HOME

Back in 2008, when I founded my brand of organizational tools and day planners (Simplified®) on the tactical concepts of simplicity, I had no idea what we were tapping into. I was simply leaning in to my own overwhelmed feelings as a businesswoman and new mom, on the quest for a simpler life. But our message caught on like wildfire. Women from all over the world were interested in the concepts and tactics we taught. Fascinated at the community developing around the brand, I started to wonder, *What is it that underlines this seemingly worldwide need for simplicity? What are we pushing against?*

The answer, I've learned, is quite simple.

We live in a world of too much.

Too much of everything.

Connection, communication, possessions, and commitments.

And in our homes, the overflow looks like *stuff*. For many of us, our homes are filled with objects: clothes, dishes, towels, personal effects, and more. We pile stuff on top of stuff. And all that stuff requires an investment from us—physical, emotional, and more—whether we realize it at the time we acquire it or much further down the road.

Our homes have the potential to drain us or fuel us. When set up and cared for optimally, our homes have the power to be transformative on a daily basis. They are where we can shut the doors, leave the rest of the world outside, and be our truest selves. I've spent a lot of time setting up homes over the years. Creating a living space especially for our family during the newborn stage, with baskets of diapers tucked into corners, books and toys within arm's reach. Creating a bedroom for two toddlers, with artwork painted by friends on their walls and favorite pajamas folded neatly in little stacks in their drawers. Crafting a room for a precious boy, who needed a quiet space all his own as he became a big-brother-times-two at once. And even before, creating a space for my own self, as a single gal in her first home, displaying photos of beloved friends and pinning concert tickets to my bulletin board.

Those special treasures (and special spaces) can be truly enjoyed only if what distracts us from them is removed. Trash. Clutter. Things that aren't beloved but are simply set on a shelf to fill a space. Outgrown clothes. Objects we spent money on and would feel guilty for donating. Hand-me-downs. Gifts. The old that has already been replaced by the new but still lives in the home.

On the flip side is the home that is magazine-worthy at all times. Clutter is kept at bay, the house is continually tidied, and most items meant to be used for living remain very untouched looking.

I sometimes tend to veer toward the magazine side of things. And I've realized that although beautiful to look at, this approach misses something important when it comes to my sense of well being (and my family's well-being). A curated and tidy home may look perfect, but is it inviting the warmth, connection, and fellowship we want to happen here? Or is it simply neat and tidy for neat and tidy's sake? Is it really lived in?

HOME IS WHERE THE HEART IS

One day, I had an experience that shook my previously held commitment to perpetual tidiness and order when I visited a friend's house. She has a whole *gaggle* of children. Their home is modestly sized and decorated in a pretty way.

But what I loved and found so inspiring about her living spaces is that they were actually *lived in*. Baskets had been gathered for toys (toys were put away when not in use but within arm's reach). Photos adorned nearly every square inch of her fridge (organized neatly but absolutely covering the space). A fish tank (and instructions for her son on how to feed the fish) lived in a corner of the kitchen.

In the living room, the coffee table had been replaced by a treasured quilt, a hand-me-down from a grandmother, perfect for tummy time and impromptu Goldfish cracker and apple juice picnics. Near the front door was a row of hooks for rain coats, jackets, and umbrellas, whatever may be needed when one felt inspired to get outside. Back in the kitchen, I didn't spot any Pinterest-perfect matching containers of salt, flour, and sugar. Instead clear glass containers held animal crackers, Cheerios, and lollipops (probably used for bribing if she's anything like me).

It was thoughtful, homey, and comfortable. It was clean and well-kept but also showed signs of life. The space inspired me to sit and stay a while, to play, and maybe to have some animal crackers. Life was all around us in that space. Plants and sort-of dead flowers picked from the weeds outside were tucked into Mason jars. Report cards were proudly displayed on bulletin boards, and family rules in imperfect handwriting spoke from shelves around the house.

It was the most beautiful smattering of real life. I was so inspired to get in the car that night and head to my own house. We moved a toy bin into our living room. Created a snack basket in the pantry (on the bottom shelf where toddlers can reach when given permission). And I dug artwork out of folders and boxes to display on our own bulletin boards. I pulled our wedding photos out and popped some into frames. I gathered books from around the house and stacked them on a shelf to remind me of my love for literature.

What a magical way to live . . . to embrace and enjoy our homes as the sacred spaces they are and to allow ourselves to be refueled by simply being here. Here, in this special space, surrounded by this imperfect, messy life, I'm so grateful. I'm grateful I learned this hard lesson.

In previous books, I've written about my love for the verse, "Be still, and know that I am God" (Psalm 46:10). In walking this journey, in undoing and untangling much of my own mess and overwhelm, I've found beauty in stillness like never before. I've listened to joy that can be only heard when the noise is quieted, savored moments that can be only seen when the pace is slowed, and experienced love that can be felt only when our focus is narrowed.

I've learned, above all, that less is truly beautiful. That happiness and contentment can't be manufactured, bought, subscribed to, or achieved by adding more to our lives. It's the counter-intuitive action of stripping away the excess that allows us to discover beauty and joy in the good lives we already have.

In walking

this journey,

I've found **BEAUTY**

in **STILLNESS** like

never before.

DEAR CAROLINE

Dear Caroline,

Here we are. But this isn't the end of my story. And it's not the end of yours. Our journeys toward becoming the girls God called us to be continue every day. It's a beautiful, perfectly imperfect process this undoing, unbecoming, and untangling ourselves from the world, this finding of more through less.

So I will leave you with this: you, my beauty, are different than you were when you first picked up this book. Now you know. You know you were made for more. With this knowledge, you have the power to choose which path you will take from here, what priorities you will place at the top of the list, and what type of life you will create for yourself.

Nothing is more beautiful than being a woman. Use every ounce of spirit and strength in you to boldly stake your claim in this world. Change is scary, but God is good. Transformation happens little by little. Dig deep into your heart, and plant this seed of truth: you are worthy, my girl. You are spirited, strong, and bold. You are never too big or too small. And you are always great, especially when you are good. Above all, my girl, be you.

Enjoy the pigeons that swipe the crust from the sky. Savor the sound of your own little one's rhythmic breaths as he or she drifts to sleep in your lap. Never forget the weight of that little body on yours. Cultivate a home that makes you feel alive, safe, and comforted. There is magic in that. Treasure music, stories, and imagination. Allow God to work His wonder in you.

No matter who you become, sweet Caroline, you are so loved. By me, by your daddy, and by your heavenly Father. He made you just right.

Love,

Mom

You are **WORTHY**, my girl.

You are **SPIRITED**,

STRONG, and **BOLD**.

You are never too big or too small.

And you are always great,

especially when you are good.

Above all, my girl, be you.

CONTINUING THE JOURNEY

Inspiration, Favorites, and More

Along the way, I've curated a selection of favorite books, songs, and ideas that inspire me to connect (and reconnect) with my desire for slower, simpler living. I hope you find the resources that follow to be uplifting, encouraging, and thought-provoking.

I've also included space for you to add to these lists so they can become special resources for you to return to when life inevitably begins to feel frantic again. Remember, the journey to less is just that: an imperfect, continual journey to living your very best life.

◾ ENCOURAGING PEOPLE *to* FOLLOW

- @erinloechner
- @sallyclarkson
- @wellwateredwomen
- @readtealeaves
- @morganharpernichols

- @simply.living.well
- @cupofjo
- @bevcooks
- @simple.slow.living
- @shereadstruth

_____

_____

_____

_____

◾ INSPIRING BOOKS *to* READ

- *Chasing Slow* by Erin Loechner
- *Only Love Today* by Rachel Macy Stafford
- *The Lifegiving Home* by Sally and Sarah Clarkson
- *Slow* by Brooke McAlary
- *Simple Matters* by Erin Boyle
- *The Little Book of Hygge* by Meik Wiking
- *Present Over Perfect* by Shauna Niequist
- *Simply Tuesday* by Emily P. Freeman

FAVORITE TRUTHS *to* LEAN ON

These are a few of my favorite verses—truths I've tucked deep in my heart for when I need them most. I hope they are encouraging to you as well.

Be still, and know that I am God.
Psalm 46:10

So do not fear, for I am with you; do not be dismayed, for I am your God. I will strengthen you and help you; I will uphold you with my righteous right hand.
Isaiah 41:10

"Come to me, all you who are weary and burdened, and I will give you rest. Take my yoke upon you and learn from me, for I am gentle and humble in heart, and you will find rest for your souls. For my yoke is easy and my burden is light."
Matthew 11:28–30

Wait for the LORD; be strong and take heart and wait for the LORD.
Psalm 27:14

■ WAYS *to* MAKE *a* HOUSE *a* HOME

I've been tasked with making our house a home five times over the course of my adulthood. In crafting our homes, I've learned that there are a few small comforts that really help evoke those special feelings of belonging, ease, and coziness. Here are a select few.

- A family calendar
- Live plants
- Children's artwork
- Photographs
- Beloved books
- Framed cards or notes from others
- Flowers (or even weeds!) from the yard
- Treats within arm's reach (a bowl of candy)
- Pressed flowers from a nature walk
- A prism hung from a window (dancing rainbows everywhere)
- Treasures displayed as decor (a favorite recipe tin, bronzed baby shoes, or your grandmother's Bible)
- Pillows and blankets near seating areas

_____

_____

_____

_____

▌ FAVORITE SONGS *to* SLOW DOWN TO

Just as decor sets the mood of a room, so too do the sounds and songs we allow to fill its space. I've created a collection of beloved songs—those that help us slow our pace, settle in, and breathe a little deeper. This playlist is perfect for soothing rushed mornings, as background music for dinnertime, or even just to slow your heart a bit after a hurried day.

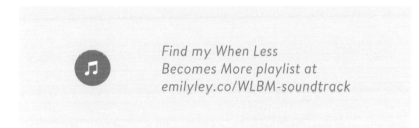

Find my When Less Becomes More playlist at emilyley.co/WLBM-soundtrack

▌ OTHER SOUND IDEAS

- White noise: the bedtime sound of choice at our house.
- Acoustic music: our family loves a good guitar song.
- Instrumental acoustic music: each of my books was written to this music.
- Audiobooks: children's audiobooks are a great way to settle lively little spirits.
- Silence: give it a try!

SIMPLE ACTIVITIES *to* DO *with* KIDS

Take a nap together in the middle of the day. Even just a few minutes of rest and conversation will do wonders.

Play outside with a water hose. The opportunities here are endless.

Find a dirt pile. Dirt piles are magical playgrounds.

Make cookies or a snack together in the kitchen. Perhaps take a blanket outside for a picnic. Or sit right down on the kitchen floor. Your kids will love the change of pace.

Lie in the grass and watch the clouds. Look for bugs in the grass. There are worlds waiting to be discovered outside.

Go for a nature walk with a small bag or bucket. Look for little treasures along the way.

Plant something, water it daily, and watch it grow.

Color. Draw. Get creative. All you need are crayons, paper, and patience.

Look through old photos together. Tell stories of when you were a child.

SPECIAL SENTIMENTS *for* KIDS

Our words have power. We can build up or tear down. With children, we have such opportunity to plant seeds of confidence and love by tenderly sharing genuine sentiments daily. I love discovering affirmations beyond the standard "I love you." The collection below includes words shared with me by my own mom, those that I've gathered to share with my kids, and a few I've overheard friends say to their little ones. What a blessing it is to be adored.

- *I love being your mom.*
- *I appreciate the big kid you're becoming.*
- *That thing you did today was brave*
- *You've made me think of things in a new way.*
- *The jobs you do around our house help our family.*
- *I love your happy heart today!*
- *Being your mom is my greatest adventure.*
- *I love spending time with you, just you.*
- *I really like hearing about your day.*
- *I'm so grateful God gave you to me.*
- *You are beautiful, even when you're unhappy.*

ACKNOWLEDGMENTS

Bryan, you've loved me through the more and the less and every-thing in between. I'm the luckiest to get to do life by your side.

Brady, you are my sunshine. My whole world changed in the most beautiful way the day you were born. When life gets complicated, come home to your mama. I love you forever.

Tyler, your spirit brightens my every day. You are delight-fully joyful, and I hope I can grow up to be more like you. I love you, TJ.

Caroline, this book is for you. I've been there, and I will love you through it when you get there. Beauties, forever.

Mom and Dad, thanks for telling me I could be anything I wanted to be when I grew up. And for always believing me when I said I'd become a writer. I still can't believe it's true, but you always knew it would be. Mom, thank you for living this journey before me—for knowing the truth in your heart, gently teaching me along the way, and allowing me to slowly and messily experience my own discoveries. To be a mother who can teach her child the way she should go, comfort her when she messes it up, and support her as she figures it out . . . I hope I can do that for my girl too.

Brett, thank you for encouraging me endlessly and always.

Gina and Ashley, thank you for allowing me to share your talents and photos in this book. Even more, thank you for believing in this message and helping me bring it to life.

Laura, MacKenzie, Jen, Mike, Stef, Hannah, and Shari, thank you for loving this book into existence and helping me launch it into the world.

Claudia, thank you for your endless guidance and direction on this journey with me.

Jessa, your art gives so much life to my words in this book. I am so grateful for all you contributed to this book baby.

Whit and McKay, thank you for allowing me to share your stories in these pages. Your words and journeys are so special.

Brittany, Whit, Hannah, Dusty, Taylor, Jessa, and Lindsey, thank you for reading these words first and helping me shape them along the way. I am so grateful for each of you.

Kristin, I love you, friend. Thanks for championing the importance of this message with me. And for all those afternoon walks.

To all our Pensacola friends, thank you for welcoming our family home.

To all the friends who let me bounce these words off of them, thank you from the bottom of my heart.

ABOUT THE AUTHOR

EMILY LEY is the founder of Simplified®, a brand of planners and organizational tools for busy women. Emily has been featured in *Forbes*, *Family Circle*, *Better Homes and Gardens*, *Glamour*, and *Good Housekeeping*. She has been recognized with numerous awards, including Best New Product at the National Stationery Show as well as Top 10 Designers to Watch by *Stationery Trends Magazine*. Emily and her team recently collaborated with AT-A-GLANCE® to create gift and planning collections carried in Office Depot, Staples, and Target. Emily is the author of national bestselling books *Grace, Not Perfection: Embracing Simplicity, Celebrating Joy* and *A Simplified Life: Tactical Tools for Intentional Living*. Emily lives in Pensacola, Florida, with her husband, Bryan, and their son Brady (8) and twins Tyler and Caroline (4).